MW00932491

AGING
OR
AGELESS?

RISE LIKE A PHOENIX FROM THE MYTH OF AGING

RON ZELLER

RonZeller.com

First Edition
Third Printing October 2014

Manufactured in the United States of America
1 3 5 7 9 10 8 6 4 2

Disclaimer: The information contained in this work is for educational purposes only. It is not provided to diagnose, prescribe, or treat any condition of the body. The information in this work should not be used as a substitute for medical counseling with a health professional. Neither the authors nor publisher accept responsibility for such use.

The materials on "be-do-have", "taking a stand", "responsibility", the "occurring world", "completing the past", "being complete", personal environment as an "existence system", "becoming nothing", "the space of all possibility", and "integrity" were originally developed by Werner Erhard and are used with the permission of the copyright owner, Landmark Worldwide LLC.

ISBN 978-1-4922-2539-3

*Dedicated to family and close friends: Ron, Susan, Rick, Michelle,
Ryan, Sarah, Tony, Nicole, Adam, and my wonderful grandchildren.
I am proud of you all!*

*To my good friend and partner in the Phoenix Project
Susan Pepus without whose support the ageless project
and book would have remained nothing more than a good idea.*

*To Peter Laubach who soloed the Badwater Ultramarathon with me,
handled the technical aspects for the creation of this book, managed the
audiovisuals of the Sundance courses in ageless living. You have been
and are a full out generous partner in transforming the myth of aging.*

*To my mentor, coach, and friend, Werner Erhard, who lit the torch
of transformation, held it high, and introduced me to possibility,
"This is it!" and a life that makes a difference. Werner is ageless.*

*And to all the Landmark Education forum leaders and staff partners
I've known through the years; you have been and are
warriors for transformation.*

*Especially dedicated to my magic elf, eternal companion, and
the love of my life, Mary Louise who co-created the Phoenix course,
who embodies the Phoenix and lives an ageless life!*

December 2013

CONTENTS

Be Ageless

THIS BOOK IS ABOUT BEING AGELESS. You can be ageless at any age, but it especially matters in the latter stages of your life. People in the United States are living longer but if you examine the quality of their lives, living longer is not necessarily such a good thing. More accurately, we could say that they are aging longer. According to recent statistics, the average American spends the last seven and one-half years of life incapacitated to some extent or rapidly going downhill with one or more destructive ailments such as diabetes, cancer, Alzheimer's disease, arthritis, heart disease, and so forth. I am interested in quality as well as length. It is now said that the rising generation will not live as long as their parents. Presently, quantity is in question as well as quality!

I am committed that you will finish this book knowing you have a say about how you experience life at any age and exceptional power to deal with the vales you pass through. At any age and under any condition, you can transform the quality of your life. At any age you can bring forth a life other than the normally accepted, probably going to happen, culturally expected predictable decline of life. There is a pathway to a World of Ageless Living.

Very ancient but still prevalent in many parts of the world, the Phoenix Myth is about aging. It contains a secret code that when used can guide us to magnify our aliveness and adventures no matter what our age. It is secret because it is so simple and straightforward.

You don't need to be lonely, feeling separate and disconnected as you get older. You don't need to be waiting for interesting events to happen in your life, or for others to notice you. You have the power to create an exciting and enlivening life at any age. Of course there will always be surprises that nobody planned on—life is an adventure, but I believe we have a lot more to say about this journey than we realize! Now let's begin your voyage to the World of Ageless Living.

The Secret Code of the Phoenix Myth

One of the world's most inspiring myths, the Phoenix Myth is thousands of years old. It has existed throughout history in different cultures and countries under different names and in different versions, but its message remains the same.

When a myth touches the consciousness of billions it is an indication that the myth resonates with who we really are and that we resonate with the message—individually and collectively. This book is about that message, discovering the Phoenix Code, looking to see how you can live it and using the Seven Keys of the Phoenix Myth to empower yourself to live the message. Using these keys, the code of the Phoenix Myth can open up a new world for you—the World of Ageless Living. You will find the message of the Phoenix Myth especially valuable if you are committed to living powerfully and fully all the years of your life.

Like many ancient myths the code of the Phoenix Myth is not clearly spelled out but can be inferred, interpreted, and deduced as you read between the lines and search for it in folklore, fairy tales, poems, and stories about the Phoenix.

In very broad strokes the main elements of the Phoenix Code are:

The immortal bird in this myth represents each and every human being—including you and me.

The Phoenix had a one-of-a-kind, unique song; so do you. The Phoenix was immortal; so are you. The Phoenix

3

dealt successfully with aging; so can you. This myth about the Phoenix actually reveals more about who you really are than your identity, personality, and ego.

The deep message of the myth that so resonates with humanity is this: At any time and under any tragic circumstance, each of us individually or all of us collectively, have the ability to transform our self and/or our environment and rise up again even greater.

When San Francisco burned to the ground during the earthquake of 1906, the citizens standing in the ashes said, "Like the Phoenix we shall rise again." The city was rebuilt more majestically than before. During the Civil War, General Sherman ordered Atlanta destroyed. The citizens of Atlanta whispered to each other, "We shall rise again." Will was mustered, choices were made, and a new city rose out of the ruins.

Drug addicts, brokenhearted men and women, business failures, alcoholics, people told by their doctors they will soon be dead, military warriors with broken bodies, accident victims, and others have declared, "These circumstances are just circumstances, and I/we shall rise again!" And they did. You can too. It's our innate power to be able to transform. It is always an inspirational journey, and I suspect the myth inspires us to give our best when we listen to the message, recognize its truth, and believe in our ability to do it!

Another main element of the Phoenix Code is the choice to see yourself as one hundred percent responsible for your experience in your world.

Are you willing to take the stand, whether realized or not, "I am cause and responsible for my experience of life." This means you give up being the victim of others and circumstances. This means you are willing to put your hands on the levers and dials of your life. This means you give up reasons and explanations for whatever doesn't work that you are aware of. This means you give up saying "you make me feel …"

When the Phoenix prayed to Ra, the sun god, for support in attaining youthfulness and got no answer, it proceeded on its own to cause its own transformation.

The Phoenix Myth contains Seven Keys for mastering your power to transform your relationship to aging. Embedded in the myth these Seven Keys tell us how to achieve transformation. This book will focus on how to rise like a Phoenix from aging to ageless. But the power of the Phoenix Myth is not limited to the transformation of aging to ageless. It also applies to moving from breakdown to breakthrough in any area of life. The power to move from the darkest moment into the light again—along with the new results that occur on the journey—I call the *Phoenix Effect*.

Briefly, the Seven Keys contained in the Phoenix Myth are:

1. Choose and commit to succeed.

This is more than "I want to" or "I would like to." This is not "I will continue only if it's comfortable and not too much work." This is not "I'll go ahead as long as I feel good about it." This is committing that you will succeed no matter what—like a vow, oath, or promise. This is to choose and commit to be unstoppable. This is also to choose to honor your word that you will be successful.

2. Complete the past.

Agelessness requires you to be complete with your past. You complete regrets, resentments, faultfinding, and persistent negative feelings such as anger, guilt, and resistance about others and yourself. You get rid of clothes and other things from the past that you cling to but no longer use. You let go of habits and behaviors that really don't serve you. Completing your past is an ongoing activity in your inner and outer space.

3. Become "Nothing."

To transform, you must go through ... nothing. It's like transmutation. To change lead into gold, you first have to **un-lead** the lead so there is space for the gold to manifest. If you look you will see we relate to each other and ourselves as **things in a world of things**. Let go of being a thing and try being space. In the Phoenix Myth, celestial fire burned up the aging Phoenix. It disappeared. What would it take to disappear *you*—your ego, your fixed way of being, your identity, even *Me*—so you can create presence, awareness, consciousness, and a clearing? You are unlimited. You are in the void. The state of nothing must be experienced not understood. From nothing what's possible is anything. We are speaking here of nothing not as an ongoing state but an occasion.

4. Create yourself.

Who would you be if you weren't stuck being *Me* or *I* but could invent yourself newly? You might invent a magnificent brand new life of extraordinary quality. Read the autobiography of American architect Richard Buckminster Fuller and get a sense of what reinventing yourself looks like. At his lowest point of self worth in life after he had lost his money and his wife's family's money in business, he transformed himself. Many of our planet's greatest inspirational leaders like Nelson Mandela created themselves newly from the depth of a life that wasn't working or looked as if it would never work.

Creating yourself is a major, major demarcation in the sands of time. It requires that you be the cause of your life rather than merely a reacting observer.

5. Cause and manifest your Phoenix future in the world.

How do you create and manifest an unpredictable future in the world with unprecedented results? How did President John F. Kennedy create and manifest a man on the moon? You'll discover how to cause and manifest an unpredictable future the same way.

6. Connection.

The best example of connection is the relationship of a mother and her newborn child. Total acceptance is present. Connection is essential for satisfying relationships in life such as community, family, intimate partnerships, and loving friendships.

Eastern tradition maintains that our later life should be spent seeking our connection with the Divine or the Universe, the Great Wisdom that directs. Many of the planet's greatest mystics assert that we are all one. Pursuing authentic communication with children of the universe (others) reveals our spiritual connection. It's almost impossible to be joyful and happy while primarily engaged in being alone and separate in life.

Sharing and communicating facilitate connection. I'm not saying to get connected by communication. I am saying to communicate from already being connected. The communication you experience when you come from being connected is not what is regarded as ***normal*** communication—the attempt to get something, resist something, fix things, or just survive.

7. Contribution.

The Phoenix Myth leaves us inspired with the possibility of overcoming and coming forth newly in the face of any circumstance—including aging. Since inspiration is the main contribution of the Phoenix, your ultimate contribution is to live a life of inspiration. Ageless people inspire others by who they are being and what they accomplish in life.

A beautiful example of the transformation of aging to ageless and the part that the key of contribution plays is found in *A Christmas Carol* by Charles Dickens. What did Scrooge do to free himself from the grip of aging? He ***de-Scrooged*** himself; he let go of stinginess and became generous. He directed his attention to the world and contributed. He made his life about what can I give (which is unlimited) not what can I get (which is limited).

Creating a World of Ageless Living for yourself leads to a life of wonder, discovery, and an unfolding future filled with glorious surprises.

Now is the opportunity to claim your extraordinary greatness. Welcome to your magnificent second half!

— *Ron Zeller*

Introduction

MY NAME IS RON ZELLER. I have trained and consulted more than 300,000 people worldwide how to transform their lives, and I'd like to empower you to deal with *aging*. Before you get started on this journey, though, I'd like to share what qualifies me to speak to you about becoming ageless.

When I was sixty years old my life wasn't pretty. I saw no future worth living for. A doctor had just told me that I would be dead in less than a year. Instead of accepting that death sentence, I chose to create a new future. I was victorious over cancer, curing myself with the assistance of a great team of nontraditional health coaches and teachers. At a medical follow-up six months later no trace of my stomach cancer could be found. My doctor said the cancer was only in temporary remission and would be back. That was twenty years ago.

My major health issue was just the beginning. At sixty-seven I lost my life's savings after heavy investing in the technology sector of the stock market. Man was I stupid! I played that game with more than I could safely afford to lose and not fully aware of the entire design of the stock market. For example I didn't know that members of Congress had access to insider trading that I legally didn't. I didn't even know what I didn't know. At my age it was a financial "death sentence." Yet just three years later I had recovered both my physical and financial well-being. I was living a great life as a successful international consultant and trainer, running ultra marathons, and enjoying my three million dollar house in Sundance, Utah, a block from the ski runs.

When I looked at my life then, a decade after my initial assessment, I realized my life was far from ordinary. At an age when most people were "retired," watching things go downhill, mine was a life of extraordinary quality. Contrary to the stereotype of retirement, my life had been one of expanding accomplishment with my advancing years. Was I doing or being something different from most people in their later years?

At seventy-two, I decided to examine my life—past, present, and future—from the perspective of *aging*. I thought about a small handful of people in my life who appeared to be *ageless*. You probably know at least one person like that: someone who is bright, clear, and active regardless of how long they've been on the planet. These are people who inspire the rest of us just by being who they are in their later years.

My mother was one of those souls. Even when her body was diagnosed as being full of cancer, and her doctor told me she had a maximum of only three months to live, she powered on for another thirty-one years. But first she posed a great question to that doctor: "Who the hell are you to tell me how long I have to live?"

You undoubtedly know someone like that. We all have heard of celebrities who live well despite their advanced age. Fitness guru Jack LaLanne was an amazing example of the full life; others would include Nelson Mandela and England's Queen Elizabeth. But there are also thousands of everyday people competing, playing, and creating, regardless of their age. When it comes to aging, they seem to march to a different drummer than most. Their bodies may get older, but their spirits do not; they have an ageless quality, and they shine. Is it just luck or do you and I have something to say about the quality of our life and our future no matter what our age? Can we cause ourselves to be Super Agers?

Along the way something happened that was nothing less than amazing to me. I wanted to know how to live outside the box of limitations associated with being old, so I signed up for a punishing hundred-mile endurance race in the Wasatch Mountains of northern Utah. During my preparation for this race, I never successfully covered more than fifteen miles in a training session—but on the day of

Wasatch 100 finish line—discovering a new me, one who can run over 100 miles

the race, with the support of an incredible team, I crossed the 100 mile finish line. I never in my wildest dreams really believed I could or would do that.

My life was never the same after that. That victory gave me the confidence to take on physical challenges beyond my believed limitations; I subsequently ran and trekked the Annapurna Range in Nepal, covering about 150 miles at high elevations in the Himalayan Mountains.

Later, taking up weight lifting in my seventies, I entered and won first place in national and world competitions in power lifting. In my life, there was no way Ron Zeller would ever be a world champion at anything, much less at raw power lifting at the age of seventy-seven! Winning at things I wasn't good at was surprising. It was surprising to discover I wasn't who I thought I was! I had unexpected powers and abilities beyond my taken for granted limits.

I wanted to share the tremendous satisfaction I was experiencing, so I became a business executive coach as well as a life coach and mentor, teaching others to deal with their aging with real power. In a course I designed and called "Winning the Second Half," I shared my experience of *being ageless* and trained others in transforming from normal living to extraordinary aliveness. The course was not about what to do, but *who to be*, a critical factor that we will see plays a huge role in our experience of aging.

What I found after years of training and inquiry was that those who are ageless view the world and themselves differently. The things they pay attention to, find important, and play around with are outside the usual mental landscape of those who are simply growing older. Those who are exceptions to the usual predictable patterns of aging, in essence, defy and ignore the *myth of aging*.

The myth of aging is pervasive. It manifests as a paradigm that dictates our behavior and shrinks the possibilities we see for ourselves as we get older. The myth about aging may be unwritten, and even unspoken, but the cultural grip on us from that shared belief is just as powerful as the flat earth myth was on people prior to Columbus' daring voyage. The myth of aging creates a self-fulfilling prophecy trapping us into being who we really aren't in our forties, fifties, sixties, and beyond. We usually become resigned to what is predictable for older people. We follow a path of comfort and give up on our dreams and unique contribution because *I am too old*. We assume a mental state that makes us receptive to illness.

In contrast to myths that deceive, such as the myth of aging, there are powerful myths that point at hidden secret realities. What we ordinarily think or believe about aging may not be the reality we have to actually face as we get older. These ancient and powerful myths still speak to us today if we are willing to look at them newly and listen for their message. Like philosophy, religion, and science, ancient universal myths have their own message about living your greatest life possible—and that includes the myth that specifically deals with aging—the Phoenix Myth.

As I researched ancient literature about aging, new beginnings, rebirth, and transformation, I discovered the extraordinary myth of the immortal Phoenix. The Phoenix Myth is thousands of years old and found in many cultures. Versions differ slightly but the message is essentially the same.

The myth tells the story of an immortal creature—a bird of fire—that wanted to do something about the circumstance of aging it was facing. The myth seems to have originated in Egypt. Basically in that version, the Phoenix finds a way with the help of Ra, the sun god, to be larger than the condition and circumstances of aging. It constructs a mirror-like nest, adopts a trusting attitude, and passes through a fiery door into nothing (***no thing***) and from there into a renewed life of youth, energy, and contribution.

Intrigued, I went to Egypt to study the culture that gave rise to the Phoenix Myth. What I learned changed my life, and it can change yours. Hidden in the myth are deep truths about our existence and our relationship to life and age. I call this the Phoenix Code and you can successfully move through one of the most difficult stages of life using the essential elements that make up this code. A code allows us to look at something in a new way that enables us to empower ourselves.

This book is about the possibility of being ageless. It's not an easy journey. The ageless life is not the norm. Our very youth oriented culture argues against a life of expanding beauty and magnificence as we get older. Instead, we live in a world with a ***known*** landscape of what it looks like to get older. As we get older we are sometimes told to "act your age" or treated as though we have nothing of value to say. You may have had or will have people speak to you in what is now called "elder-speak," as though you can no longer understand what's going on around you or as if you were a child.

Now in my eightieth year, I declare there is another world—the World of Ageless Living, one that is filled with magic, glory, and surprises. This book is about helping you discover that world and its possibility—how to give yourself more power, not less, as the years go by. You can become a master of Being Ageless.

First, let's begin with a fundamental assertion—***there is nothing you have to fix about you***. Who you are underneath the façade of the false mindset of *Me* is already perfect. This book will help you discover who you really are and, in the process, empower you to deal with aging in a way you never knew possible.

How to Get the Most from This Book

To get the most from any endeavor, begin with commitment and full engagement. Along the way to accomplishment, there are circumstances that rise up in opposition. They will either stop you or, if you overcome them, strengthen you.

Commitment provides the overruling power to keep going in the face of external circumstances like losing your job, experiencing a death in the family, going through a divorce, or enduring the negative comments of family and friends. Being committed trumps your automatically occurring internal landscape—such as doubts, thoughts, feelings, and limiting self-talk—that argues for procrastination, quitting, and possibly even permanent defeat.

Commitment is the first essential element powerful enough to transform a paradigm—in this case, the unforgiving paradigm of aging. In his book, *The Scottish Himalayan Expedition,* author W. H. Murray captures the power of commitment with these words:

Concerning all acts of initiative and creation,
there is one elementary truth, the ignorance of
which kills countless ideas and splendid plans:
that the moment one definitely commits oneself,
then, providence moves too. A whole stream
of events issues from the decision, raising in one's
favor all manner of unforeseen incidents,
meetings and material assistance, which
no man would have dreamt would come his way.
I have learned a deep respect for one of Goethe's couplets:
Whatever you can do or dream you can, begin it.
Boldness has genius, power and magic in it!

Once committed to master being youthful at any age, begin to live the Phoenix Code, including the Seven Keys. Determine how you can integrate the message of the Phoenix Myth into your life. For example, one of the Seven Keys of the Phoenix Myth is completion. Ask yourself, "In what area of my life am I not complete?" Then do the work to complete those things, and watch them disappear from your life. You will start to notice yourself living with an unusual energy we call the Phoenix Effect.

The Phoenix Effect is a way of *being* that leaves you with an elevated ability to interact newly with life at any age, especially when it all turns to trash. It allows you to more effectively deal with life when it isn't going the way you want it to go and to have a greater success rate in getting life to go the way you want it to go. You are in the flow— when living from the Phoenix Effect you are creating your life rather than reacting your way through life!

Few are able to overcome their past or diverge from their normal way of living. In this book, you are guided to decipher the Phoenix Code and the Seven Keys contained in the code that enable you to escape your predictable, limiting future.

You don't have to figure anything out or even understand the code. Just allow the hidden message of the Phoenix Myth to emerge and new views of reality to impact you. This will give rise to your full self-expression throughout all the areas of your life to the highest degree possible for the rest of your life.

Living this coded message requires that you be complete with your past. This is covered in detail in the chapter entitled "Completion—Burn Up Your Past and Fly to Freedom." There is work to be done. The stakes are high—your life!

As you complete your past, you create a blank slate upon which you may write new possibilities for your future. A newly created you, like a Phoenix, rises from the ashes of your past and lives brightly the rest of your life.

Often it might seem as if I am repeating myself in this book. Well I am! The Phoenix Code will be presented in many different ways and from different points of view. Educational research has shown that this type of repetition and reiteration helps you better retain what you're learning. The design of the presentation in this book, then, deepens your power to make this message your own and use it instead of merely understand it.

Most of us have a lot of partially read books sitting on our shelves. You will need to finish this book and apply the principles of the Phoenix Code if you want to open the door to being ageless and live a youthful life. Again, it's not easy. Aging is like a 600-pound gorilla on your back, and it represents a battle for the quality of the rest of your life! Are you going to win the second half of your game? If you do, the rest of your life can be the best of your life!

To have a new life requires that you **create** a new life and act on that new life by believing that the story of the Phoenix is really about you. Be willing to invent an extraordinary life for yourself, and begin to do the work necessary to make it happen. This is the first element of the code. This story of the Phoenix Myth is about you. You are the Phoenix. What is said about the Phoenix in this myth applies to you!

To get the most from this book:

1. Choose to live an ageless life then commit to your choice. Choose also what you want to *be*, *do*, *have*, and *give* as part of your ageless life.

2. Take on this point of view: this story of the Phoenix is really about you.
3. Stand for having the power to break free of your ordinary limits and live an extraordinary, ageless life.
4. Create Impossible Games™ that light you up and inspire you as you play them. Play as if winning is possible.
5. Transform your life from reacting to causing.

Ready to get started? I believe that you are. If you weren't, you wouldn't be reading these words. Let's begin with the story about how I got involved in becoming ageless and began to live from the Phoenix Myth.

Let's see how one might deal with hitting bottom!

PART I

Start Your Journey from Aging to Ageless

I N THIS BOOK, chapters have been combined into sections called "Parts." Part I has the theme of beginning the transformation from the World of Aging to the World of Ageless Living.

In the first chapter, I share with you a time when it really looked bad for my life, and I unconsciously stumbled on a major part of the Phoenix Myth—I can consciously cause or manifest in life as opposed to being a victim in life. Life is very complex, and we can live as if it is just happening to us, and we react in turn with automatic reactions. In this model for living we are just another thing in a universe of things, coping as best we can. There is another possible model to live from: ***I am responsible/cause of my experience/ reaction to everything that exists in my world!***

By responsible, I don't mean shame, blame, or any other added meaning. I simply mean willing to ***be*** cause—i.e. cause of any and all matters in your life (and I am not saying you really are). If you want to examine the model of "being cause in your life" in depth, the model is beautifully clarified in the book *Zero Limits* by Joe Vitale and Ihaleakala Hew Len.

This part of the code "being cause in your life," as part of a new model for your life to look and live from, will produce benefits worth over ten thousand times whatever you have paid for this book.

The second chapter of Part I explores the World of Aging that we find ourselves entrapped in. This culture of aging shapes and dictates who we will be as we get older and we actively reinforce this on each other. The flat earth myth shaped most humans' relationship to the oceans. Very few sailed more than a few miles from shore. The myth of aging is a limiting myth. It hypnotizes us into an false view of the reality of our possibilities and freedom as we get older. We become chained to our past. The past now defines our present and future. What future? Only more of the past is available. Who each of us is and can be, especially when getting older, is shaped by the culture of aging, the collective agreement each one of us lives embedded in.

The third chapter explores the nature of myths, and the Phoenix Myth in particular, to reveal hidden power we innately have to deal with growing older. This myth is one of the few myths to specifically deal with aging, and I suggest it has a deep and liberating message.

Now, let's begin your adventure…

CHAPTER 1

Staying Alive When Faced With Death

It ain't over till it's over.

— Yogi Berra

THE FIRST TIME I felt the pain in my stomach, I was out for my morning run. The year was 1992. For years, I had been exercising much more than the average person; I ate what I thought was an extraordinarily healthy diet, I did not smoke or drink, and I had been blessed with outstanding health and vitality. A mild pain in my stomach did not seem to be cause for alarm.

Four days later the pain was still there—and actually it had gotten a bit worse. I went to the drugstore to get some

Tums, yet the pain only got worse over the next few weeks. I finally went to see a doctor.

The doctor said it was probably inflammation from an infection and prescribed Tagamet. Soon the pain became intolerable; I would wake up during the night and realize I had been crying in my sleep because of the pain. I had a very demanding work schedule as a world trainer in self-development in addition to all of the ordinary requirements of life as a husband and father, and the pain made it difficult for me to continue my normal routine.

I decided I should get another opinion from an expert. My insurance required a referral from a primary care physician, so I couldn't see a specialist for three weeks. The specialist's office staff then cancelled two subsequent appointments, and I was left hanging with the pain and uncertainty. I sucked it up and endured.

About two months later, I was traveling by shuttle from my home in Benicia, California to the San Francisco airport for a flight to Boston, where I was scheduled to lead a training program for two hundred people. Very suddenly a thought pressed into my consciousness: *If I go on this trip, I am going to die!* I tried to push the thought out of my mind and discount it, but my body knew it was going to die if I continued on this trip. Yet even with these powerful intuitive warnings, I pushed ahead and boarded the plane for Boston.

An hour into the flight, I experienced excruciating pain in my stomach. My body literally panicked—it just froze.

It took everything I had to override my body's terror. To which should I listen—my mind or my body?

My body won. As soon as the plane landed, I called my company's CEO, Harry, and told him about the pain, my fear, and how I needed to know what was wrong with me. He told me to catch the next flight back to San Francisco and see a doctor.

When I landed, I called Vaughn Feather, a good friend of mine who lived at Pebble Beach in Carmel, California. Within an hour he had lined up an appointment for me to see a top specialist at the San Francisco Medical Center. It was a slightly disturbing but learning experience: Vaughn was worth billions, and he could instantly get a first-rate appointment when I hadn't been able to get one in two months. I went directly from the airport to the medical center.

I realized a profound fact that has since served me in many different domains of life: ***It often helps to identify the problem before you can effectively deal with it.*** I had to push through my reluctance to confront knowing what was wrong. I realized I had been afraid to know, because it might be bad. But by the time I arrived at the San Francisco Medical Center, the need to know overpowered my fear of knowing. I got out of the taxi and went to discover my future.

A renowned gastroenterologist performed a gastroscopy, a procedure in which a camera is lowered into your stomach. He told me I had a very large ulcer over the vagus vein that appeared as if it was about to burst. He told me if the vein ruptured, even if I was in a hospital at the time, the odds were that I would die. He recommended an immediate course of treatment. I didn't argue with that.

During the gastroscopy, it was standard procedure to take random biopsies—tissue samples. A week later the doctor called me with the results of the tests. Examination of the tissues showed a severe cellular anomaly in the stomach lining around the ulcer. More tests were required. My wife and I were subsequently called into his office to discuss the results of those tests, which indicated that I possibly had cancer of the stomach.

Michael, my gastroenterologist, recommended me to an oncologist, a cancer treatment specialist. The oncologist went over my latest test results from a lab at Stanford Medical Center. Bad News! Cancer. Terror rushed in and my mind was filled with thoughts of terrible futures.

He recommended a protocol of treatments including an operation, chemotherapy, and radiation. With each recommended treatment he also spoke of the associated and calculated percentage risk of death and severe side effects. Combined, the risk of death added up to more than 100 percent—not the kind of odds that sounded good to me. So I asked, "What if I do nothing?" He replied, "At the very most, you might live a year."

As I listened to his matter-of-fact pronouncements, the wave of terror swept over me—a year or less to live! Oh My God!

My view of life shifted in that moment.

The doctor asked, "When would you like to begin treatment?"

"I am not going to begin treatment," I replied. That reply surprised even me! Looking him in the eyes I said, "I am going to die a natural death." With that pronouncement I got up to leave.

"You're crazy!" the doctor screamed at me.

The truth was I didn't trust Western medicine to successfully deal with this kind of health breakdown. I didn't trust that Western doctors really know what they are doing when it comes to cancer treatment. They practice *hope* medicine. In hope medicine they hope that what doesn't work for 97% of those treated will work for you. I wasn't about to simply turn my health and life over to well-meaning doctors and then hope for the best. A good friend of mine, actor Raul Julia, had the same kind of cancer. He followed the recommended Western medicine cancer protocol and soon died. I suspect it was as much from the treatments as from the actual illness.

I wasn't going to allow the doctors to hasten my death and intensify my suffering by poisoning me with leftover World War I mustard gas, burning me with radiation, and cutting out a large portion of my stomach. It didn't seem like a logical way to recover my health. Incidentally, twenty years later, the results of standard Western cancer treatment protocols are still not reliably working to restore people's health; the survival rates found 31,500 women treated for stage 4 breast cancer, only 2% survived past year 5. A poor return for the terrible quality of life most cancer patients report. A poor return on all the pink marches, pink fund raisers, breast cancer runs, and all the activity around breast cancer. Someday that fact will be confronted by all of us. Medical research might discover a cure if we looked in a new place.

My reaction to the doctor's recommendations seemed to trigger a rage in him. He probably was not used to someone questioning his authority and confidence. As far as I saw it, though, I was simply declining his sales proposition. He certainly was not neutral about my decision. After all, all the T.V. pharmaceutical ads counsel us to "ask your doctor." According to them, you certainly should never make a choice about your own body without your doctor's approval!

The Oncologist followed us out of his office and into the hall spewing sarcastic and insulting remarks about how stupid I was and telling me that I would kill myself. Actually, strangely I felt really quite powerful; I knew I was doing the right thing. *Screw you and your $300,000 cancer treatment that will definitely make me suffer and then kill me*, I thought to myself. My wife and I walked out of that building into a new world—a world in which I was now dying of cancer.

When I walked out of that doctor's office with Mary Louise, I realized I was truly on my own. In a way, it would have been so much easier to turn myself over to the doctors and just do what they said to do. Being complacent and agreeable seemed like the proper way to be, and following their advice the only thing to do—what everyone would expect was the reasonable and sane thing for me to do. At that moment, it was as if I was suddenly lost—like I had landed in some unrecognizable, alien world. At the same time, I just knew that **I was the ultimate one to cause my own healing and health**. That realization was the first step in my journey back to well-being and vitality. I still use the standard medical community for many health issues, but I knew this wouldn't be one of them.

Of course I am only sharing my journey and each one of us is unique. I was righteous and positional about my view. I am not there anymore. There are powerful new alternative therapies slowly being discovered outside of the burn, poison, and cut business model of cancer treatment. There are many dedicated doctors committed to curing cancer, however there is a money driven system that is engaged in keeping things the same.

The first few days of assuming full responsibility for the management of my painful disease and my very survival were terrifying. Yet I told myself that I would have time to settle my affairs, enjoy each day, and fully appreciate life in a way in which I couldn't if I died suddenly in an accident. Oddly enough, while I felt reassured and in charge of my destiny, I was still terrified.

After rejecting the normal medical protocol, I quit almost everything familiar. I resigned from my satisfying work in transformative education with Erhard Seminars

Training, known as "est," that had defined me for twenty years. Abandoning all of my normal and familiar daily activities, I found myself in the strange experience of the unknown—a land of **uncertainty**. Nothing was **normal**, but strangely enough, I felt power to truly create something new. It seems that along with taking responsibility comes the opportunity to create.

I began to create a plan to die a natural death. This wasn't exactly familiar territory. It had been natural to plan for the future, and I had done that all my life. I was an obsessive planner but didn't exactly know how, or want to learn how, to plan for my death.

Mary Louise and I talked. I told her that I had always wanted to travel the whole country and I thought now might be the only time. Our son Adam, born to us late in life, was only four and not yet in school. This could be an extraordinary time, this last year of mine, to be together in a way in which we had never before been. That's what we chose to do. We sold our home, gave away or sold all our **stuff**, bought a new Ford Diesel Dually that we named **Growler**, and bought a Canadian Triple E fifth-wheel trailer. Mary Louise and I had the windows tinted and our rig strikingly customized. It looked like something out of Star Wars. Even when dying, it seems to be very important to look good! We set off with our four-year-old to see the good old United States of America. It would be one hell of a dying journey in our Darth Vader rig!

A week into the dying trip I was talking by phone with a friend, Laura, who shared that she had recovered from a similar condition by going on a ***healing journey***. Laura had sold her home and traveled around the world exploring natural cures for her cancer. She said that she had made her whole life about healing herself and had succeeded. She was now well and cancer free. That day I shifted the context of my trip from a ***dying journey*** to a ***healing journey***.

After talking to Laura, I found myself having new thoughts and a less morose outlook on everything. It was even possible to conceive of being well one day—vibrant, vital, and energetic again, something I had just taken for granted my whole life. My healing plan was to super-charge my immune system and trust it to deal with the lymphoma. My friend and work associate, Stewart Esposito, once said, "When you don't know what to do, do everything." I decided to follow his advice. I would put off the Western Medical cancer treatment to the end though.

I began by learning about the lymph and immune systems and talking to people who had overcome cancer. Normally Western medicine categorizes any disappearance of cancer outside the customary medical treatments as a "spontaneous remission." They seem to assert that anyone who ever recovered from cancer without using a prescribed standard medical treatment had absolutely nothing to do with his or her own healing. It must have been an ***act of God*** or some sort of unexplainable ***fluke***, maybe even a misdiagnosis. I decided to find more of the people who dared to act outside the box and healed themselves. I vowed to listen to them as if we have the power to cause our own healing. That is exactly what I did.

This mindset gave me access to new and unique ways of looking at my situation. From that point forward, my journey became an adventure of recovery, reinvention, and living. I would be like the fabled Phoenix bird rising from the ashes! Many years later, I would study this Phoenix Myth in depth and find hidden within it Seven Keys that open up the possibility of ageless living for us. That's what this book is about: our power to rise from the ashes of our circumstances into a glorious new world.

After one lesson in a church parking lot on how to drive and operate our magnificent and highly technical thirty-three-foot R.V., Mary Louise and I packed our luxurious big rig with just the essentials and set off on the first leg of our journey. We headed for Los Angeles.

For weeks we had studied all about full-time R.V. traveling. One of the first rules of the road was repeated over and over: Never arrive in a big city during rush hour traffic. We got to L.A. at 5 p.m. A crazed L.A. commuter, swerving from lane to lane, clipped the back end of our R.V.

We had an accident our very first day on the road!

The nut didn't even stop! He took off! The damage was minor, but we learned the hard way that our R.V. driving manual and all the videos we watched were right on.

As we traveled east through the United States day after day, we began to feel competent in our new self-contained world. Mary Louise had worked as a field service engineer for a national medical supply company and had repaired microscopes and photo-micrographic

The start of a dying journey—you have to stay alive to be ageless

equipment for years. She had training in electronics, optics, and mechanics. That was a good thing. Mary Louise climbed under the trailer many times and rewired electronic components that had failed. A trailer is bigger than a microscope, but the electronics are sometimes similar. It worked to have a mechanical mind aboard our new rig. Mechanical was definitely not my forte. Good thing I married well!

As we traveled down the highways of America, one of us would drive and the other would read to and teach Adam. Adam learned to read prolifically on that trip and is an above-average reader to this day. Every afternoon about four, we pulled into an R.V. park and settled in for the night. Adam pulled his bicycle out from under the basement storage area of our R.V. and went in search of kids to play with. We inevitably ended up at the pool and Adam played with his new friends for a couple of hours. We had an extremely varied experience: some of the R.V. parks we found were five-star resorts, while a few were close to trailer trash pit stops.

Days after our near fiasco in Los Angeles, a very stressful first day to say the least, we arrived in Dallas, Texas. A friend and work colleague had told me about an extraordinary healer in Dallas by the name of Dr. Dohyun Choi. Dr. Choi had healed Pope John Paul II after he had been shot in the stomach in an attempted assassination. The best of Western medicine had failed to heal the pope's wound. Dr. Choi had a long history of making a difference with health issues like cancer when Western medicine hadn't been successful.

Impressed by these success stories, I engaged Dr. Choi for a two-week course of therapy.

Dr. Choi worked with my energy fields using the Korean healing modality of acupressure. The treatment consisted of nothing more than simple touch but when I left Dallas, my pain was mostly gone! I felt that the radical change in my pain was a very strong indication that something had happened.

Also during our travels I met Clarion Chandler, a certified Indian medicine woman whose medical license on the wall was a piece of deerskin signed by fourteen Indian chiefs. Clarion was a massage therapist and the walls of her home in Sedona, Arizona were covered with original works of art—oil, colored pencil, watercolor, and charcoal pictures of masters, sages, and prophets of all countries, times, and cultures. Clarion worked on me for several days and I can honestly say that it exceeded any massage therapy I could imagine.

You should know that I am a scientist by training; I received my master's degree from Brigham Young University in geology. I worked as a geologist for the U.S. Atomic Energy Commission and for several universities. At the University of California, Berkeley, I worked in earthquake research under the great pioneer in that field, Dr. Bruce Bolt.

Coming from my ingrained scientific world view, what happened during the massage Clarion gave me can only be described as mind blowing! I had to let go of my normal understanding of reality—my mindset, my frames of reference, my world view—and just be with the experience. The massage left me in wonder and enabled me to let go of all of my health concerns.

During the massage, I had conscious experiences of being another person in another body at another time. In one of those experiences, I was a gladiator in an arena and actually smelled dust and blood. I was hearing the screams of terror and rage. I smelled death. Out of nowhere, a spear was thrust into my stomach. I was even aware that Mary Louise was there as a fellow warrior. As I lay there, mortally wounded, I looked up and watched as Mary Louise went on fighting for her own survival, leaving me to die alone! Reasonably, that would be a smart move in the heat of battle, yet my perception was that she abandoned me. Interestingly, I have always had an underlying sense of being abandoned by her. She can go shopping, go get her nails done, or even be working diligently for the family, and I experience abandonment. Strange, isn't it?

My next experience during the massage was being the captain of a battle-engaged starship. During this future time a laser smashed through the hull and hit me in the stomach, exactly where the spear had penetrated—and, surprisingly, in the exact site of the cancer.

Finally, I was aware of my existence, somewhere in a glorious crystal palace with spectrums of multicolored light and energy swirling all around me. In the background I could hear Clarion chanting and praying to the Great Spirit to heal me of all injuries sustained in this area of my body—injuries from the past, the present, and the future. Normally I would not tell anyone this happened. Too bizarre!

Our adventure together that afternoon took me outside of the scientific, objective paradigm I had so self-assuredly dwelled in most of my life; it dumped me into a peaceful alternate new reality—not as a conceptual tourist, but in a lasting and life-altering experiential way. The work we did together amplified the fundamental core issues of my eternal being. I don't know how else to say it; it was one of the most profoundly awakening experiences of my life in terms of realizing who I really am—beyond the work I did in life, the family I had, or even who I had always thought I was. The grip of the illusion of being a thing in time and space was relaxed.

I have heard it said that the American Indians have long regarded the white man as not complete human beings. I became a ***whole human being*** that day as we finished our work together. Everything changed, expanded, and realigned after that work with Clarion Chandler. Even my relationship with Mary Louise totally transformed; we became deeply connected at the level of Being. Our love evolved to an eternal connection, deepening and expanding. Who knows how or what happened; I just know something happened to heal a lot more than my body. This became a healing journey beyond what I could have planned or even imagined, taking me on the ride of my life.

After leaving Sedona, I made a quick trip back to San Francisco and spent time with Victor, a physicist with the Russian KGB, who obviously does not want to be identified.

Victor could see inside the body and move energies around in a health-enhancing way. He didn't speak much English and I don't know if his treatments did any good but Laura had highly recommended him.

Also included in my healing journey were Randy McNamara and other members of the Landmark Education Forum Leader body, people with whom I had worked for years as an est trainer and later as a Landmark Education international trainer. The company est was one of the first organizations dedicated to training large groups in transformational education. Werner Erhard, who created est, is one of my most revered mentors. Landmark Education was the child of est and was a supportive structure for dealing with my life-threatening health breakdown. From my relationship with the people at Landmark I learned another valuable lesson for dealing with serious illness: If you ever find yourself in a similar situation, look around and use the resources of your whole world to help heal yourself.

My healing journey also included colon therapy and spending time with Tom and Flame Lutes in Colorado. They helped me complete suppressed feelings and emotions. We worked together for several extraordinary days during which I experienced healing and expansion. At this point in my healing journey I felt whole and complete and had no pain. I felt tremendously blessed.

Following yet another recommendation by a friend, we drove to Florida, where we spent three months at the Hippocrates Health Institute just outside West Palm Beach. Just a mile away from Hippocrates, we found a beautiful shady R.V. park that was off the main road. Hippocrates turned out to be an elegant Spanish villa with lovely gardens and grounds. Their ozone-purified swimming pool gave the feeling of swimming in silk, unlike the harsh chlorine-treated water of most other pools. The healing protocol of this health institute is based on the work of the great healing master Ann Wigmore, a Latvian who popularized wheat grass juice, sprouts, and an organic diet of live, raw fruits and vegetables to restore health.

Ann Wigmore also had an institute in Puerto Rico, where I flew to work with her personally. A simple yet profound and creative woman, she had been taught by her grandmother and introduced me to the power of raw foods and exercise to reverse health breakdowns. In Puerto Rico I lived on wheat grass juice and a literal banquet of raw gourmet fruit and vegetable preparations, including "energy soup," a live raw green vegetable soup. For breakfast we ate raw sprouted buckwheat cereal with raw shredded apples and cinnamon. I spent hours running and walking on the beach and swimming in the ocean. Best of all, I still had no pain and was feeling increasingly more alive. The energy soup was working; I had more energy than I had felt in years. I understood that I wasn't fighting cancer; instead, I was providing the real nutrition that my body needed to be alive and well.

It may sound strange, but I spent long hours meditating, accepting the cancer, and asking my body to teach me what it needed to heal itself. As I look back, having cancer was probably the most powerful learning experience of my life. Of course, I am not asking for another lesson in that school.

In addition to my health issues, my wife Mary Louise was going through her own Phoenix experience–a total disruption in her life before moving on to powerful new self-expression.

During the previous three years, Mary Louise had been studying the martial arts. Our son had had an accident when he was eighteen months old. He recovered quickly, but Mary Louise didn't. She was diagnosed with posttraumatic stress disorder and struggled and suffered for months after Adam's accident. She enrolled in a Taekwondo school to recover her fitness and courage for life, and her only regret in leaving California was having to leave her Taekwondo school and Master Kim, who had empowered her profoundly.

Mary Louise was forty-four when Adam was born and had suffered four miscarriages in the process of getting that guy across the bridge. She had always been athletic, but between the miscarriages and the accident, she was in the worst shape of her life. Taekwondo literally brought her back to life. She was thrilled to find out that she could continue her study and strengthening with Taekwondo as we traveled.

Each evening whenever we arrived in a new R.V. park, she would look in the phone book for an Olympic Sport Taekwondo school and call them to see if she could train with them for a few days. They always graciously invited her to train without charge. It turned out to be an incredible opportunity to learn from different masters across the country and greatly expanded her knowledge and skill. It was truly a rare opportunity. She found a particularly good Taekwondo school just one mile from the R.V. park in West Palm Beach and enrolled Adam in an afternoon kindergarten program next door to the studio so that he could enjoy himself while she trained. Adam even took a children's class in Taekwondo. It was perfect, and we were all thriving. I was feeling stronger and more vital and alive than I had in years.

We decided to continue our adventure and headed north. Mary Louise grew up in Atlanta, Georgia, and we stayed a month and visited Mary Louise's family, enjoying the striking beauty of springtime in Atlanta.

At the strong urging of Mary Louise, I flew back to San Francisco Medical Center to undergo follow-up medical tests to determine the status of the cancer. My gastroenterologist was astounded when a gastroscopy failed to show any sign of cancer. He biopsied my stomach extensively—probably to show me the error of my ways and have me return for the chemotherapy, surgery, and radiation the oncologist had recommended. I think he was not only frustrated and confused with the new results, but was probably disappointed. I asked him if he wanted to know what I had done to heal myself. He answered, "No, we can't do or recommend any of that anecdotal healing nonsense. That cancer probably hasn't gone anywhere; we just haven't found it!"

I have discovered I can count on many doctors to stick to their medical protocols, no matter what reality is staring them in the face. His gloom-and-doom prediction that the cancer would return seemed surreal; I felt it insulted my determination to be responsible for my own healing. More than that though, it assured me that I was on the right path. Again I walked out of a doctor's office, leaving him to deal with the unprecedented predicament of having to resolve the conflict between reality and dogma. I also don't claim my experience is typical—I know many great dedicated doctors.

As I write, that episode of my life is far in the past. The cancer didn't come back. I have never gone back to that doctor. I think the disappointment and disillusionment of knowing that I am still healthy and well twenty years later might be a lot for him to handle. The oncologist had said I would be dead in a year without the typical cutting, poisoning, and burning treatments. Fortunately for me, his prediction was wrong. Again, I want to make sure you know that I am not maligning doctors—my son Ryan and his wife are doctors—but I don't mind pointing at the present "acceptable" cancer treatments as deeply questionable regarding their effectiveness for most of us.

During my meditations, I thanked the cancer for the lessons it taught me. In fact, during my healing journey, I made it a point to relate to my cancer as a teacher, not an enemy—not as an internal alien that had to be poisoned, burned, and cut out. Cancer taught me to be aware of my body and to give it living fuel, pure water, strengthening exercise, and rest. At that point, I acknowledged my cancer as having accomplished its mission and invited it to leave. It did. I am well. It's easy to fall into a stressful mindset of a fight and battle when dealing with serious health issues. But I didn't find that the common way of seeing our health breakdowns as fights, battles, and wars left me peaceful. I believe being peaceful is conducive to healing.

As this new world of healing opened up for me, spiritually and physically, I discovered that I could be powerful in the face of overwhelming and terrifying circumstances in all the areas of my life. Dramatic improvement in the quality of my life emerged, especially the day I chose to recommit myself to having my life be about making a difference, serving, and being a contribution in life.

Before I got sick, I had first worked in traditional education as a university teaching assistant, junior high teacher, high school teacher, counselor, junior high and high school principal, and superintendent of a private school system in California. I then went to work in the newly developing field of transformative education. I trained and coached people to produce real breakthroughs in their lives—breakthroughs that brought forth unprecedented power and success for them. As mentioned, I had worked with est and Landmark Education as a Trainer and

Landmark Forum leader and with Werner Erhard, a master in creating and generating transformational models. In my experience, empowering people to live fully self-expressed is a high level of service that makes a difference. After many years as a traditional educator, my work in transformative education gave me access to extraordinary opportunities for service, contribution, and empowerment. I experienced the privilege of earning my livelihood by making a difference in the quality of life for tens of thousands of people around the planet. I was profoundly satisfied and fulfilled with my life and my work.

When I finally realized that I was not going to soon die, at least not from this stomach cancer, Adam was six years old and we were camped at a campground in Provo Canyon, Utah. We decided to settle down. We bought a house two months later. Mary Louise enrolled in a new Taekwondo school and registered Adam for the first grade. We were again building a future together. I found a way to contribute and serve again by teaching transformative communication.

How did I stay alive when they told me I was going to die soon? This is what I would tell a friend:

> You need to identify the problem as best you can before you can effectively deal with it. Then find others who have had this problem and successfully dealt with it. Learn from them some possible ways you might deal with it.

Realize you are the One. You have the power to cause your own healing. It is up to you. Use all the resources you can find.

Shift the context. See a life-threatening illness not as dying but as a healing and learning journey. It is a healing journey of body, mind, and spirit.

When you don't know what to do, do everything according to your light, intuition, and inner wisdom.

On your healing journey and with any serious life issue, step outside of your individual separate view and use the resources of your world.

Dramatically shift your practices and actions. Small measures are a good start but keep going.

Flood your body with nutrition and enzymes from live raw organic foods.

Eliminate poisons and toxins in a variety of ways, such as skin brushing, a liver cleanse, sweating, and colon cleansing. Eliminate mental toxins such as guilt, stress, blame, regrets, and emotions like fear and anger.

Keep reducing stress. Find ways to feel better emotionally. Discover what activities and adventures in the present and in the future will bring you joy.

Finally, find a doctor or several you can trust.

But even if you survive the many diseases that threaten you, there is one disease that nails virtually every one of us: AGING! If you want to know how to most effectively deal with *that* one, keep reading!

CHAPTER 2

Escaping the Myth of Aging

I was not happy about coming down with aging.
It made healing myself of cancer look easy.

— Ron Zeller

IN 2004, after defeating cancer, I realized I had another very serious illness—*aging*. It's a worldwide epidemic. Everyone seems to catch it as they get older. Since many people have it and almost everyone will get it, we already know a lot about it, having been conditioned by society as to what its characteristics are. Without even being aware of it, we live in a culture that includes the paradigm of aging, and this all-pervasive paradigm engulfs and contains us as we grow older. Have you ever heard of **living in the box**? The box gets smaller with the passage of time.

As I took a look at it, I quickly determined that the decline of life comes with a paradigm of the World of Aging. It wasn't a world in which I wanted to live. It certainly didn't look like fun, nor did it seem to be another adventure. At that moment, I consciously chose and committed to discover how to live life outside the World of Aging.

For most of us, aging doesn't show up as something we can alter; instead, it shows up for us as an inevitable part of life. It also doesn't seem to be something about which we have a choice. Based on our limited view, we all engage in judgments, stories, and conclusions about the way aging is. We make automatic, reasonable decisions on how to live as we get older. Even saying "I am too old" starts reducing your options and choices. Your mind starts to **believe** that you are and will be aging "normally." Your feelings argue for the reality of our beliefs about aging. You become more embedded in the myth of aging. You are bewitched by human herd consciousness into being old before our time. You think like an old person, move like an old person, and seek more and more comfort.

Our agreed-upon World of Aging is another pervasive paradigm that correlates with a fundamentally flawed mindset of human being as a thing. This paradigm is universally accepted as the real and only World of Aging—when, in fact, it is actually a **culture** of aging, a human condition of agreement. There is a powerful **story** about aging that we tell ourselves, tell others, and even pass down to our children. It is a story that physical and mental decline accompanies aging. That story appears to be real, when it is actually a powerful myth. But this mindset is an all-pervasive context that leads to a self-fulfilling prophecy! Think about it. What is the common story about aging in our culture? What is **real** for you about getting older? When it comes to **being old**, what do you consider to be absolutely true? Mind trumps body. Whatever your fundamental thinking about aging is, it will begin to rule your body.

Consider some of the words we use and hold to be true in describing the World of Aging. While there may be some exceptions, the old adage that the exception proves the rule applies. As we age, we think it is normal to retire, be less productive, get physically weaker, and lose the ability to do all that we have loved to do. Don't you think it is a squandering of well-earned wisdom and experience to be "put out to pasture" just when you've learned a few things? To start with, we expect to some degree to lose our faculties; get fat, bald, wrinkled, ugly, and forgetful; lose our physical senses, like seeing and hearing; lose our health. We become sexless, lonely, and powerless; to no longer have goals; and to put up with others discounting and discarding us as we grow older.

People have even invented another language called **elder speak**—they speak more loudly and simply to the elderly, assuming that their ability to understand is diminished.

Some of the notions that exist in the folklore refer to what will happen to your body, some refer to how others will relate to you, some describe the diminishment of life, and some speak to the conditions you will face with aging.

When Julie Andrews turned 69 she commemorated her birthday on October 1, 2009, with a special appearance at Manhattan's Radio City Music Hall for the benefit of AARP, the American Association of Retired People. One of the musical numbers she performed was "My Favorite Things" from the legendary classic, *The Sound of Music*. Here are the actual lyrics she sang:

Maalox and nose drops and needles for knitting, walkers and handrails and new dental fittings, bundles of magazines tied up in string—these are a few of my favorite things.

Cadillacs and cataracts, hearing aids and glasses, Polident and Fixodent and false teeth in glasses, pacemakers, golf carts, and porches with swings— these are a few of my favorite things.

When the pipes leak, when the bones creak, when the knees go bad, I simply remember my favorite things—and then I don't feel so bad.

Hot tea and crumpets and corn pads for bunions, no spicy hot food or food cooked with onions, bathrobes and heating pads and hot meals they bring—these are a few of my favorite things. Back pains, confused brains, and no need for sinnin', thin bones and fractures and hair that is thinnin'—and we won't mention our short, shrunken frames—when we remember our favorite things.

When the joints ache, when the hips break, when the eyes grow dim—then I remember the great life I've had—and then I don't feel so bad!

Ms. Andrews received a standing ovation that lasted for more than four minutes, with the audience demanding repeated encores. She put a voice to the World of Aging as we know it. But—is that world the only possibility?

When I started to contemplate aging as a ***disease***, I saw consistent patterns of automatic and unquestioned ways of thinking regarding aging. The way that I thought about aging was not unique; it was most definitely a cultural paradigm in which I existed, along with the rest of us. Unexamined paradigms determine the thoughts you can have, limit what you can feel and cause behavior consistent with those thoughts and feelings. I noticed it was not just how I related to aging, but virtually how all human beings relate to aging. This culture of aging reinforces our view of aging—including the agreed-upon perceived limits to what is acceptable and normal behavior. In some cultures elders are appreciated, honored, and venerated as they get older. This is not normally the case in our culture.

How you see aging shapes every aspect of your life as you grow older—finances, sex, health, family, energy, and aliveness. You consciously and unconsciously agree that you are too old to have more adventure or accomplish the extraordinary. You may settle for living life vicariously, watching more TV, and seeking to be *entertained* by life instead of *living* it. You become a spectator in life, because being old equals living on the sidelines for most people. The untold lie in this scenario is that inside this shared view of aging these confines are largely self-imposed. This environment, the way others live as they grow older, reinforces and creates a World of Aging.

While there are people who do not live in this World of Aging, they are few and far between and seem a bit like freaks. They include people like magician Harry Houdini's manager, who at the age of a hundred and five was waiting tables and running five miles a day. We still have **Blue Zones** or places on our planet where there are high concentrations of elders who are healthy and strong despite advanced age and the aging stereotypes. Jack LaLanne claimed that healthy eating and consistent exercise had given him the high quality of life he had up until the age of ninety-six, when he suddenly passed away. He demonstrated we have something to say about the quality of our life as we get older.

Most of us know older people who are amazing—people who don't fit inside the World of Aging.

We have agreed in our culture that there is a very narrow age zone when you are just the right age—probably between twenty-five and forty. But when we examine this view in detail, it begins to look ridiculous. We are discounting most of our lives based on a superstition! This World of Aging that we buy into is not real. In our culture, this emphasis on our younger years being the best was made up, perpetuated, and now is real and inescapable. I am committed that by the time you finish this book, you will have created the possibility of having the rest of your life be the best of your life.

Why Do We Limit Ourselves As We Get Older?

No one knows the future, yet we unthinkingly try to predict, control, and force a certain future outcome. Our brains are actually prediction machines, the function of which is to predict and control the future, enabling us to continue to live consistent with our past and what we already know. The purpose of this mechanism is to ensure our survival as a thing by having our past and the world as we know it survive. All of this adds up to good news—but not for you if you are looking for a higher quality of life at any age.

This might sound odd, but the concern about aging can strike at different ages. Some of us catch it at forty, others at fifty, and still others at thirty. Regardless of how old we are, at some point most people start to relate to themselves as too old and not as ... as I used to be. They have entered the World of Aging. Of course there are different rules for living successfully in each era of life.

Just as each of us catch aging at different times, each of us deals with the onset of aging in different ways. Some of us automatically give up, accepting the decline and diseases of aging as concrete limitations. At the opposite end of the spectrum are those few who manage to live great lives of adventure and possibility, no matter their age or state of health. They choose to resist aging or just live life on their terms. They make the best of it.

One of the most powerful examples I've seen of those few who are ageless was at the 2002 Winter Olympics in Salt Lake City. The man who carried the Olympic torch down Main Street toward Eccles Stadium for the opening ceremonies had a fatal illness that would kill him later the same day, yet he carried the torch proudly, high overhead. It is a torch that represents the best in all of us to be great. He had trained and prepared himself to carry this heavy torch as an example of the Olympic spirit. My guess is that he died very satisfied with his final day. On that day he was ageless.

With that same general spirit, I decided to confront aging like I had confronted the illness of cancer. I decided to be proactive and responsible instead of sitting around and letting aging do its thing to me. I was not going to be a victim; I would be my own doctor and cure myself.

We will all experience physical aging and death, yet the ordinary mental and spiritual decline associated with aging is only one possible choice. You can choose to fight to be well and strong with every breath of life, a choice that includes the choice of transformation from the normal decline of aging to agelessness. I've named the results from this transformational process the ***Phoenix Effect***. The name represents the fact that like the Phoenix, an individual or community is renewed, reborn newly and will rise up even greater. Like the mythical Phoenix, we can rise again from the experience of aging—not just to the same way of being, but rise anew as a newly youthful, magnificent, immortal being. The ***being*** part of human being has been virtually unexplored, yet it is through the power of being that we may access a life of unimaginable possibility at any age. The Phoenix Effect isn't just about recovering a new life in the face of aging. The Phoenix Effect is also about a new beginning in the face of any major breakdown.

Having been an educator most of my life, I decided to create a course to teach others what I had learned and was learning on my journey from aging to ageless. Drawing on my background in transformative education, I decided to transform the disempowering culture of aging. I committed to a future where we all have the freedom to be well, engaged in high performance, and singing our unique song regardless of our age.

For eight years, Mary Louise and I researched, developed, and led a course that we called *Transforming the Myth of Aging*. This course was not about tips, prescriptions, and recipes for getting better as we grow older; it was about accessing the power of being in order to be ageless. The course caused a transformation in the experience of aging that shaped behavior, deepened understanding, and provided new knowledge. We have seen astounding and miraculous results in those who have attended the program. We found much gold by digging deeper into who we all are being when it comes to our age. The *being* of human being has been virtually unexplored; it is there we planted our stake in the ground.

Seven Keys are included in the Phoenix Code. Using these keys you may change who you think you are regarding aging, how you view aging, and what is possible for you in your life regardless of your age. These Seven Keys enable you to cause, design, and plan the rest of your life to be the best of your life while sailing through the murky, stormy waters of aging.

I want to come at this aging experience you and I have from a few other directions. By so doing, we will expand our view from an aging mindset to include how we know what we know about existence, reality, and the world. Warning—this is heavy going, but it is rewarding because it frees us from being caught up in the circumstances of aging.

As human beings, we live in a world that we call *reality*. If we get outside our process for knowing this so-called reality and question it, we discover that who we think we are, who we think others are, the world we see, and even what we believe possible is actually a function of how reality occurs for us. Each of us has a set of assumptions, core beliefs, thoughts, and habit patterns that ruthlessly perpetuate an unconscious and consciously unquestioned, limited view of reality. Of course there are many different cultures on the planet, but mostly we resign ourselves to the culture in which we find ourselves. Now we are left with only a partial—and therefore inaccurate—view of reality.

There is a cost to living from a distorted view. That cost includes the loss of your freedom to take powerful action to realize your dreams, especially as you get older. Your self-expression, greatness, and magnificence become blocked. You don't know what you are capable of. You have enormous power you never call on. This unused power could make a dramatic difference in your life as you age if you draw upon it to deal with life when things are going badly.

For example, Doris "Granny D" Haddock got tired of political corruption and decided to walk across the United States to protest it—*in her ninetieth year*. A couple of years later, she decided to run for Congress and she almost got elected. "Granny D" was an inspiration as she empowered herself and escaped from the box of aging.

Although we feel as if we intelligently and rationally observe our world and phenomenon of aging, our view is actually determined by a paradigm that literally creates the world view we perceive. We then unconsciously consent to a personal reality extracted from our limited mental view. Our individual limited view likely has nothing at all to do with reality and everything to do with our personally accrued sets of beliefs, thoughts, and emotions from the past.

I am not saying you should believe what I am saying, but I would like you to consider that the normal *culture* of aging does not constitute the *reality* of aging except by agreement. In other words, if everyone agrees that something is a certain way, it becomes temporarily real until they agree on something else.

There's another factor: Consider the existing culture of aging. That culture—a paradigm of reality shared by a large group of people who have some commonality—defines the reality of what it means to grow old, and it is brutally suppressive. Our culture dictates our experience of aging by conditioning us to accept the superstition of what it means to grow old. Stop for a moment and consider the paradigm of aging in which you live. What do you really know about what it means to be old?

After the age of thirty, each decade results in most people getting slower, weaker, fatter, grayer, and more wrinkled. At some level we are concerned that what happens to others will predictably happen to us. It seems inevitable that we will lose our vitality, our health, and the ability to do the things we love the most.

Those are the physical effects of aging. But there are substantial emotional effects as well. As we age, we may regret what our lives could have been, and we regret not having accomplished most of our dreams. While young, we often substitute making a living for living our dreams. As the years advance, we determine that life has passed us by and it's too late for us. Because we *believe* it's too late to live our greatest chapters in life, it actually *becomes* too late. We *believe* that who we are is our physical body—a body that will get feeble, get sick, and eventually die. That view diminishes our power to live more fully as the years go by. Let's take an opposite point of view—are you willing to have your greatest chapters of life in your future? Are you willing to step outside of your body and say, like a Phoenix, "I'm ageless"? Are you willing to have your mind rule your body?

To further reinforce what we already know about aging, we live in a culture that idolizes youth and discards the richness of wisdom born in experience. In this culture, virtually everyone not only believes, but **is**, "Who I am is my physical body, and this body will deteriorate as I get older. I will get feeble, get sick, and die." This view of reality in which you are a thing diminishes your power to live more fully as years go by. *Things* age and get older, and we have been inaccurately considered in Newtonian physics as **things**. Are you willing to be like a Phoenix and be other than another **thing**? Are you willing to be an immortal being with a body?

To experience the Phoenix Effect, first discover that the decline associated with aging is a choice—a choice in which you can decline to decline! I am convinced that aging, as we presently know it, is to a large extent a powerful superstition, a view of life that limits us to the degree to which we buy into it.

In our work, we have proven that, like the Phoenix, you can choose to reinvent yourself and create an unpredictable new future. You can disassemble and complete your past—a past based on unconscious reactions, regrets, and resentments that then create interpretations of reality and self-limiting mindsets about you and others. You can powerfully bring yourself forth as an ageless, magnificent being. You will find that if you give up those unreal self-limiting interpretations, you will be left with a space in which you can create a new future and a new way of being, including actions that enable you to deal with life at any age.

Do you still have a physical body for which you are responsible? Absolutely! But if you view yourself as ageless instead of as the hopeless victim of aging, you will take on that responsibility with enthusiasm and authority.

From the Phoenix Myth, we have discovered a new world—the World of Ageless Living—a 180-degree departure from the illusionary World of Aging. If you dare to enter this exciting new world, you will be exploring and pioneering a new World of Ageless Living possibility for yourself and others. Along with others who are blazing the trail, you can now choose to join the mission.

By reading this book, you are now standing at the portal to the World of Ageless Living. Your demand to enter this world will be the first step in a remarkable odyssey into the unknown. It's worth the price. It takes courageous audacity to question your culturally conditioned view—a view in which you complacently think you know who you are and that you know your inevitable future.

Beginning the Journey to the World of Ageless Living

The first developmental stage of our present work was entitled "Winning the Second Half." Participants in that seminar were able to break out of their normal mindsets about themselves, age, and aging. They also broke through lifelong self-limiting patterns and ways of being. They invented new futures and determined what it would take to be the person who lived those futures. Many of those first participants are now unrecognizable to themselves and others. They have accomplished unprecedented results and effective new ways of being in every domain of their lives. People were empowered to be who they had never imagined they could be. It worked!

Interestingly enough, we most often think about what we *don't* want in life. Too often, even when we look at what we *do* want, we just don't believe that we have the personal power to bring those desires and dreams into reality. It's actually easier to complain about things not being the way we want rather than to create what we do want. But the people who attended these seminars reported positive changes in their relationships, their finances, their health and well-being, their careers, and the overall quality of their life and happiness. In essence, their life's visions were being realized.

After five years of further development, I began to study the global myth of the Phoenix and found hidden keys that unlock the new World of Ageless Living. This book will provide you with those secret keys and the code to make more sense of their message. You can create for yourself a pivotal experiential event that will enable you to have the life of your dreams, now and in the future.

This is not a self-improvement book. Self-improvement is linear and is fueled by prescriptions for success. Have you noticed how well that works? The magazines published each month are all about that. Considering how much they publish about losing weight, it's amazing that we are not a nation of skeletons. But understanding about how to lose weight does not provide enough power to actually lose weight. We often substitute understanding for effective action.

You deserve freedom and a life that is beyond the predictable, whatever your age, whatever your circumstances may be. Like the Phoenix, you can choose to create a new life. Instead of just reading about a life-altering process, you can immerse yourself in living from the Phoenix Code which includes mastering the Seven Keys. Even when older, you can actually be all you have ever dreamed you could be, and more. As Frank Sinatra sang, "The best is yet to come ..."

The prelude to a Phoenix Effect in your life is the creation of a new view of who you are. This is a quantum leap from the normal ***thing*** view of yourself—for example, "I am my body"—to a removed view of yourself—"I have a body." In the myth of the Phoenix, the Phoenix periodically completes its attachment to its old physical body and creates a new body, each time more energetic and youthful than before. But where is the Phoenix between bodies?

As an exercise, say, "Who I am *is* the space in which my life occurs." Say it until you can crack open merely being a thing and notice you have no age! All the enlightened ones have said and continue to say, "We are not merely bodies that get older and die. We are so much more."

It is impossible to be an advocate of breakthroughs for your brothers and sisters and not demand them of yourself. In the eight-year process of inventing and refining this work, Mary Louise and I have personally and continuously enjoyed extraordinary experiences ourselves while our lives transformed. In fact, we're not the same people we were just a few years ago. This ongoing expansion at our age is certainly not consistent with the common culture of aging.

Let me give you a few examples. In 2009, at the age of seventy-six, I led the first Landmark Education Forum, a global transformational course, in Lebanon. In 2010, at the age of seventy-seven, I won four gold medals in my age and weight division in the World Raw Power Lifting Championships. I broke four world records and four national records. Twelve weeks earlier, I wasn't even training in power lifting. Five years earlier when I first conceived of winning a world championship, I was about as strong as a weak thirteen-year-old girl. My point is, we have more available power than we realize at any age!

In 2010, I completed "The Badwater" solo, considered by many to be the hardest 135-mile ultra-marathon; it is held in the desert of Death Valley in July when temperatures average between 120 and 130 degrees. Later in the year, I took a 750-mile trip along the Salmon River and throughout Idaho on my Harley Hog.

Mary Louise, my wife and partner in this project of transforming from aging to ageless, has now been inducted into the U.S. Martial Arts Hall of Fame. As a sixth-degree black belt, twenty-time U.S. National Champion, and nine-time World Champion, she has been training with the greatest Masters of Taekwondo in the United States and Korea to complete her seventh degree. At the age of sixty-seven, she became a U.S. National Taekwondo Technical Team member after winning national team trials.

Hers is not just a physical transformation. Before her breakthrough in the "Transforming the Myth of Aging" seminar, Mary Louise was irresponsible with money; she'd look at me and say, "I am so good at spending money and you're so very good at making money—where is the

Mary Louise sparing with Grandmaster Joon Rhee, her advocate to include her on the U.S. National Taekwondo Team

problem?" I never laughed. While I traveled extensively for work, she never bothered paying the bills; I had to hire a graduate accounting student to pay the bills and manage the finances in my absence.

Now Mary Louise manages all of the finances—and does a better job than the graduate student I hired. She is currently generating financial wealth for us with international network marketing in eight countries. Talk about being unrecognizable! While she supports our family, manages our home impeccably, and even packs for my trips and drives me to the airport, her income now exceeds that of many executives. She says it is her joy to take the

No longer broke!

pressure off me and give me the freedom I have always given her. Our lives today are like a fairy tale especially when compared to my dying in a cold trailer somewhere, old, broken, and broke.

I have been at the bottom. I have known hopeless and helpless and old besides. The key questions for me now are, "How can I share with you in a way that opens up your access to having an extraordinary life? How can I support you in *living* an ageless life? How can I contribute this new body of knowledge to you and others, giving everyday access to an unlimited, ageless, and joyful world?" I believe the example of the Phoenix from the Phoenix Myth holds the answers to those questions. Isn't it great to realize we all have an inherent nature that allows for creating a new life, even in the face of the myth of aging?

Are you ready to live the life of your dreams and start now? Are you willing to dissect and scrutinize everything you believe about aging, yourself, others, life, and even what's possible in life? Then you must find the courage to go beyond the World of Aging, which is commonly accepted, into the World of Ageless Living—a new world of possibility at any age. Unless you reinvent yourself, the same limitations will always confine you.

The Chinese have a saying: "If we don't change the direction we are headed, we are liable to end up where we are going."

Actions

Answer the following questions and record any insights. I suggest starting a "Phoenix journal" where you can record your answers, notes, thoughts, ideas, etc. This can be any type of journal that you like to work with: a physical notebook, an iPad, a computer, or any other system of your choice.

1. What is the difference between the World of Aging and the World of Ageless Living?

2. How do you presently determine what is real (in actuality, not theory)?

3. Where does all you know about aging come from?

4. Given your present relationship to aging, what does your probable/predictable future of your life look like?

CHAPTER 3

The Phoenix Myth

In the Garden of Paradise,
beneath the Tree of Knowledge,
bloomed a rose bush.
Here, in the first rose, a bird was born.
His flight was like the flashing of light,
his plumage was beauteous,
and his song ravishing.

— Hans Christian Andersen

The Power of Myth

IN 1974, I participated with Czech psychiatrist Stanislov Grof in a workshop called *The Power of Myth*. We were gathered at the house of my friend, Dr. Leo Zeff, in Bolinas Bay, just north of San Francisco on the Pacific coast. The participants were mostly educators from the San Francisco Bay area who gathered at Leo's for a weekend once a month, and we always had an extraordinary experience.

A great educational psychologist as well as a psychiatrist, Leo did leading-edge research that was definitely outside the current realm of medical thought. He thought **outside the box**, which is what enables advancement. Dr. Grof brought his own expertise to the workshop. One of the founders of transpersonal psychology, he uses extraordinary states of consciousness to explore healing, health, and creative growth. He has written many books on the power of alterned conciousness to heal us physically and emotionally.

Compared to most of our sessions with Leo, this particular session was rather academic and a little tame. Nonetheless, it was fascinating to learn that some of the universal myths of human beings contain clearer pictures of reality than what we have been conditioned to believe is real.

I had always thought **myth** meant something untrue and unreal. But I was so wrong! Some powerful, lasting, deep myths actually reveal more about us and our human condition than do science, philosophy, religion, and especially our common sense.

Dr. Joseph Campbell, a global pioneer in the study of myths, once said, "Myth is the secret opening through which the inexhaustible energies of the cosmos pour into the human cultural manifestation. Great myths touch the core of our being. In these universally enduring legends, transforming truths are often disguised within the stories of mythology. If you unravel the secret code of a myth, you can claim the treasure of the hidden wisdom therein."

Let's look at that idea a little more closely. A few rare myths allow us to expand our view of life, opening up new possibilities and new ways of being. These myths provide a unique means of viewing ourselves from within humanity's collective unconsciousness. The result is far more powerful than simply looking at ourselves from our individualized points of view. Instead, we're able to see ourselves from outside our normal blind spots—blind spots that keep us embedded in limitation, delusion, and ordinariness.

Simply put, a great myth is a traditional, timeless story about heroes or supernatural beings. Such myths often illuminate origins of natural phenomena or aspects of human behavior normally imperceptible and indistinguishable. Myths also often answer fundamental questions about our very existence through folklore. As one example, the entire 3,000-year-old Egyptian civilization was founded on a single detailed culture-shaping myth about creation. My fascination with mythology began that day in our weekend at Bolinas Bay California.

Even though the great myths give answers to life's deepest questions, the term myth is often trivialized to mean nothing more than a superstition or mistaken view of reality. You've likely heard people say, "Oh, that's just a myth."

There's no doubt that myths are sometimes generated to purposely distort reality. Following the 9/11 disaster of 2001, a myth about terrorists was created that many Americans now live inside of. It's actually not too different from the politically motivated myth of the 1950s that there is a communist behind every tree.

What happens when we dissect that myth? On September 11, 2001, a group of what seemed to us to be fanatical foreign zealots attacked the United States and killed more than 3,000 of our citizens. That was a tragic event. But look at what has happened since: A whole new culture of reaction to the myth of terrorism has dominated our lives since 2001—something that is arguably even ***more*** terrible while not making us any safer. We are now victims of a pervasive national myth with a view of reality that says we can protect ourselves from future attacks by tightly controlling our own citizens, eliminating long-standing freedoms, and attacking and dominating people of other countries and cultures. We are multiplying the damage of the original attack by bankrupting ourselves and justifying inhumane practices against innocent bystanders.

As a nation we currently spend a large percent of our national budget on "defense." In other words, fear dictates our national actions and attention. Pushing a myth about a danger beyond proportion allows the government to avoid transparency and accountability by keeping citizens off-guard and frightened.

To the people of many other countries, we Americans are the terrorists with our smart bombs, drones, and other engines of war. Our government's policy of continuously engaging in military conflicts drives us trillions of dollars into debt. As a nation we have sacrificed and continue to squander our national wealth and human resources largely in response to the politically maintained terrorist myth. It's a myth that's especially useful to some special-interest groups. And those who question this fear-driven course of action are largely demeaned and viewed as un-American. This myth allows for political control and extraordinary financial gain for military contractors.

To further illustrate the limiting aspects of some cultural myths, let's consider the premise that we as human beings naturally and unconsciously generate interpretations of life that become all-encompassing mindsets. Each of us lives inside our own myth of what is real. What is real to any of us is the "myth of Me"—and it's the biggest illusionary myth of all.

We each dwell in fixed, unchangeable, and enduring perspectives that create in our minds an unreal world in which we exist. Within that world, our mindsets determine our views. Aging—and the way we age—is just one example of such a mindset.

The human part of a human being is our physical body. Examining the human condition more profoundly, we discover that we actually live in an illusion: "I *am* my body." This illusion is so pervasive, we don't see it; it is like water to a fish. In defense against this fundamental premise, we might respond, "Of course I know I'm not my body"—but consider the profound fear that automatically arises at the thought of injuring or losing your body. When you are asked, "How are you?" You most likely will explain how your body feels.

In addition, we place a lot of priority on any emotions our body chemically produces in any moment, as well as the thoughts automatically generated by our brain. We normally identify with whatever is happening to us physically in our body i.e. our feelings, thoughts, and emotions. It is all as random as the weather. It's just happening. We are that who we are—are all of these thoughts, feelings, and bodily sensations.

Let's look at this another way. We live inside of and are being used by a world view—not reality, but a view of reality. In this view, we experience that we exist in relationship to a world of physical things and then assume that human beings, therefore, are also just physical things. We then naturally relate to ourselves and each other as things, reinforcing this illusory reality of who we consider ourselves to be—a bunch of things, always striving to get those other things to be and do what we think they should be and do. We think if we could just get those other things to be and do what we think they should be and do, we would be happy. Through observation from birth, we have learned that this is how life is—and if we are to succeed in life, we must become masterful at getting others to be and do as we want them to be and do. Most of us try to master domination and manipulation and we call it love and power. It never occurs to us that the view that we are all things is merrily an illusion of our Western culture.

As long as I can remember, I have experienced being a thing that only knew who I was by comparing myself to other things. If other human things were shorter, I was a tall thing. If some things were older things, I was a younger thing. And I have certainly tried to be a good thing in contrast to all the bad things running around out there.

Things are defined and located in time and space. So where do you find this thing called Me? If I ask you to point to yourself, you will probably point at your chest or head. If I ask you how old you are, you will tell me the age of your body—and sometimes you will lie about the age of your body. It is ubiquitously assumed that you are this body. We relate to each other as if each of us is our body. We relate to each other from the point of view, "I am a thing, separate from all the other things." But are you really this Me thing? If not—aging is a myth.

The Phoenix Myth

Odd as it may sound, we can use a myth to break out of the myth of aging and arrive at being ageless. Our antidote to the myth of aging is the Phoenix Myth, a myth that has persisted for three thousand years in almost every major culture of the world.

The Phoenix Myth is a metaphor for human transformation; it defines who we are and provides the steps that allow us to break loose from our linear World of Aging. If you haven't already done so, search the Internet for the Phoenix Myth. Familiarize yourself with the different versions of this myth. If you haven't already done so, stop reading now and do it.

Note what the Phoenix is, what it does, and what it has. Write a summary of what you find rather than simply trying to remember. I suggest that you use your Phoenix journal to record your notes and answers.

The Phoenix is …

The Phoenix does …

The Phoenix has …

The characteristics of the Phoenix are …

It's natural for us to invent perspectives and superstitions. The problem is that most of our perspectives keep us limited. The power of myths is that they allow us to get outside of our self-limiting mindsets and give us a choice about reinventing our lives. Broad and all-encompassing myths allow us to expand our awareness of reality and point to who we really are. An in-depth inquiry into the Phoenix Myth allows each of us to look at our world in a new way and to more clearly see the truth of our being.

Like most enduring universal myths, the Phoenix Myth contains a code or ancient messages that, when deciphered, grant access to your hidden innate powers. This code includes Seven Keys that allow you to open the door to a life of new possibility and power. That doesn't mean there's anything wrong with your life right now; it simply means that you have an enormous ability to reinvent your life. *Are you willing to transform who you normally are for the possibility of who you could be?*

Within the code, there is actually a prelude and work to be done prior to mastering the Seven Keys. For starters, consider the fact that *you* are a myth! Let's start by looking at your myth of *Me*.

Who or what do *you* say you are?

What do *you* say are your limits?

When did *you* decide that about yourself?

With your answers, you begin to know how you wound up being you. And the Me you've put together—the one you know and love so well—is a myth! The Phoenix is more real! Consider a few simple things: The Phoenix realizes it is not its body; it has a body. You are not your body; you have a body. The Phoenix knows it is an immortal being that transcends its body. Are you willing to conclude the same thing about yourself? By being immortal, I don't mean simply being a thing that lives a long time. Some people are willing to believe they are immortal, yet the experience of immortality remains elusive and foreign. To grasp your immortal self, you need to see yourself in a new way—especially when the whole conversation on this planet is that we are all things. Are you only a product of this planet? What about our universe?

The Phoenix is a one of a kind, unique individual, yet it is also a *space*—a space of renewal, hope, and new possibility in the physical dimension. You are also unique and one of a kind. As Buckminster Fuller, the famous American architect said:

"Never forget that you are one of a kind. Never forget that if there weren't any need for you in all your uniqueness to be on this earth, you wouldn't be here in the first place."

If this sounds strange, say into a mirror several times until it is real for you "I am unique and one of a kind."

You are also the space of your experience—a space of consciousness and awareness. In this space, everything you are aware of appears. As you master the distinction "I am the Phoenix this myth is talking about," you find yourself standing with a foot in each universe, the physical and the nonphysical.

Aging is a property of a physical body existing in the physical universe. But in the all-inclusive universe that contains things, energy, and the defining space in between, we are ageless. To recognize both universes gives you the power to create your relationship to age. In this new World of Ageless Living, you can create an extraordinary life—a life free of the constraints of your past, of age, and of aging. You create this life by speaking it into existence. As you speak it, you create *being ageless*.

We all live in a world of superstition about aging—a world that leaves us confined to the physical. It is a global superstition that has been unconsciously and pervasively passed from one generation to another and has simply become accepted as the way life is. The decline associated with aging exists as part of the fabric of life, and instead of being considered a superstition, it is accepted as real.

The erroneous belief that I am aging is the antithesis of our existence as immortal beings. You are not the victim of aging! Aging refers only to the physical aspect, not the being part of human being. Human beings invent from the domain of being, which is different than positive thinking. "I am ageless" is a powerful declaration of who you are being, a declaration that can generate a new world of experience and results. Inventing a new possible reality, "I am ageless," transforms your relationship to your body from *I am this body* to *I have this body*. The fountain of youth is between your ears! Now go back to your mirror and declare to the person in the mirror "I am ageless," until it rings true for you.

With nothing more than your *choice* and your commitment to live an ageless and limitless life, you can embark on a new and exciting odyssey into an unimaginable life of aliveness, creation, and self-realization. At any age, you can literally bring forth the rest of your life as the best of your life. We are not talking about adding more years to your life, but more life to your years!

The invention of your new life requires first choosing and committing to create a new life. If you want to be youthful despite the age of your body, you must choose to discover how to cause that, and you must take action to bring forth the results you want.

Exercise

To begin to use the Phoenix Code, assume the point of view that this Phoenix Myth is really about me. Consider what you see about yourself when you do this. One example could be, "The Phoenix is immortal, so I am immortal." Another could be, "The Phoenix was a one of a kind, so I must also be unique and one of a kind."

Read through the following poem from the point of view you are the Phoenix to discover yourself newly.

The Phoenix Bird
by Hans Christian Andersen

In the Garden of Paradise,
beneath the Tree of Knowledge,
bloomed a rose bush.
Here, in the first rose, a bird was born.
His flight was like the flashing of light,
his plumage was beauteous,
and his song ravishing.

But when Eve plucked the fruit of the tree of
knowledge of good and evil,
when she and Adam were driven from Paradise,
there fell from the flaming sword of the cherub
a spark into the nest of the bird,
which blazed up forthwith.

The bird perished in the flames;
but from the red egg in the nest there fluttered aloft
a new one the one solitary
Phoenix bird.
The fable tells that he dwells in Arabia,
and that every hundred years, he burns himself to
death in his nest;

But each time a new Phoenix,
the only one in the world,

rises up from the red egg.
The bird flutters round us,
swift as light,
beauteous in color,
charming in song.

When a mother sits by her infant's cradle,
he stands on the pillow,
and, with his wings,
forms a glory around the infant's head.
He flies through the chamber of content,
and brings sunshine into it,
and the violets on the humble table smell doubly
sweet.

But the Phoenix is not the bird of Arabia alone.
He wings his way in the glimmer of the Northern
Lights
over the plains of Lapland,
and hops among the yellow flowers
in the short Greenland summer.

Beneath the copper mountains of Fablun,
and England's coal mines, he flies,
in the shape of a dusty moth,
over the hymnbook that rests on the knees of the
pious miner.
On a lotus leaf he floats

down the sacred waters of the Ganges,
and the eye of the Hindu maid gleams bright when
she beholds him.

The Phoenix bird, dost thou not know him?
The Bird of Paradise,
the holy swan of song!
On the car of Thespis he sat in the guise of a
chattering raven, and flapped his black wings,
smeared with the lees of wine;
over the sounding harp of Iceland
swept the swan's red beak;
on Shakespeare's shoulder he sat
in the guise of Odin's raven,
and whispered in the poet's ear
"Immortality!"
and at the minstrels' feast he fluttered through the
halls of the Wartburg.

The Phoenix bird, dost thou not know him?
He sang to thee the Marseillaise,
and thou kissedst the pen that fell from his wing;
he came in the radiance of Paradise,
and perchance
thou didst turn away from him,
towards the sparrow who sat
with tinsel on his wings.

The Bird of Paradise-
renewed each century
born in flame,
ending in flame!
Thy picture,
in a golden frame,
hangs in the halls of the rich,
but thou thyself often fliest around,
lonely and disregarded,
a myth—
"The Phoenix of Arabia."

In Paradise,
when thou wert born in the first rose,
beneath the Tree of Knowledge,
thou receivedst a kiss,
and thy right name was given thee—
thy name,
Poetry.

There is a hidden message in the Phoenix Myth. A message that has inspired humankind for millennia. Whenever a city or nation has been destroyed by war, calamity, or destructive acts of nature, the message of this myth comes to the rescue as people declare:

Like the Phoenix, we will rise again!

How many times has this message been used as a symbol of hope? "Like the Phoenix, we will rise again!" was the impassioned cry of the people of San Francisco, providing hope and inspiration to rebuild their beautiful city following the earthquake and fires of 1906. Since ancient times, survivors sitting in ashes of devastated cities and countries around the world have called on each other to once more take heart, clear out the debris, clean up the filthy mess, and design a new environment. "Like the Phoenix, we will rise again!" was their rallying cry.

The word **Phoenix** has come to mean a supremely rare and unexpected entity that arises new from the destruction of a former self. Burning up toxic circumstances, it becomes full of more beauty and color with each resurrection. Those who find themselves devastated can borrow the spirit of the Phoenix to deal with despair and resignation, knowing they can resurrect from their circumstances. They believe it is possible to rise again. They know that our human spirit does not have to despair or give up. This points at the message of the Phoenix Myth.

When we transfigure ourselves—whether alone or with others—we have realized the Phoenix Effect. We all have this eternal spirit of indomitable will and courage. It's part of who we are.

Can you think of a time when you became stronger out of adversity? Was there a time in your life when you triumphed and emerged strengthened?

I would suggest that like the Phoenix, you can choose to rise up into a reinvented magnificent new expression of yourself, regardless of your past mistakes, circumstances, or wreckage. The Phoenix Code implies that we all are like a Phoenix in reality.

Your spirit is bigger than old age. You are ageless! You can rise like a Phoenix from the dark, hopeless circumstances that often attend advancing age. Who you really are is bigger than the age of your body or the circumstances in which you find yourself. And you can go beyond merely recovering yourself—you can go towards glory, always dancing to your own unique special song—***being ageless***.

Take a moment to reflect, "Where in life am I selling out on life's greatest adventures? Where am I not fully expressing my love, my creativity, or my commitment to my ideals? What payoffs or benefits have I gotten from doing this? What counterfeit benefits have seduced me— benefits like being right, avoiding responsibility, or being comfortable? What are the costs or losses for selling out on myself?" When you ask yourself these questions, what do you realize about you and your life? I suggest that you take some time right now to ponder these questions and capture your realizations in your Phoenix journal.

You have now been introduced to the Phoenix Myth. You have also been introduced to the myth of ***Me*** and the myth of aging. By now you can recognize that you have been looking at the world, at others, and at your own life as if your view is ***real***, when, in fact, it is only one possible view and that particular view creates your reality. Your brain has automatically maintained these familiar patterns that you identify as yourself—patterns of beliefs, thoughts, attitudes, feelings, views, and mindsets, all of which serve to maintain the continuing illusion—the myth of Me. The myth of Me generates a reaction that leaves you stuck in habitual and limiting patterns. You can break free from the myth of Me and bring forth an unrecognizable and new you.

The way out is to create. You have the power to create. I know you have the power to create because you have created and maintained the myth of Me. Now you can choose to create a magnificent life. I must warn you: In order to escape the myth of Me, you must sacrifice your ordinary *way of being*.

> Are you willing to be sponged out,
> erased, cancelled,
> made nothing?
> Are you willing to be made nothing?
> dipped into oblivion?
> If not, you will never really change.
>
> — D. H. Lawrence, *Phoenix*

Actions

Complete the following. Use your Phoenix journal to capture your notes and insights. Don't worry about trying to apply this or fix anything. Just become aware and present to the unfolding conversation.

1. Complete all the exercises in this chapter.

2. Begin to look at aging in our culture. Notice the assumptions, beliefs, thoughts, feelings, and behaviors that go along with getting older. What does everyone know about getting older?

3. How do others use age as an excuse, and how do they limit themselves because of their age?

4. Look for older people who are being ageless. Find people for whom age appears transparent and isn't an issue. List ten people you consider to be undefined by their age, except in the context of how extraordinary they are for their age.

5. Notice all the people who are resigned to aging as if it is an inescapable factor. These are people who have given up on life and who have stopped playing big, exciting games because they are too old. Imagine what their life could be like if they were living an ageless life.

PART II

Capturing the Phoenix!

I N PART II OF THIS BOOK, we look at the Phoenix Code and begin to look at the Seven Keys of this myth in greater detail.

Chapter four is about the Phoenix Effect, its stages, and the surprising results that you get when you begin to live life from the insights this myth provides.

Chapter five is about the first key necessary to bring into existence an ageless life. It's about the key of choice. Without choice, everything that happens is just an accident.

In this chapter you will experience choosing and make your commitment to an ageless life.

In chapter six, you inquire into who you are consistently being now. You will discover that you have invented a myth about yourself, the myth of Me, which you hold to be the truth about yourself. This structure of Me once in place, is designed for surviving or staying the same all the time. It becomes very difficult to change yourself even though you can.

While in chapter six you discover who you are not, chapter seven is an opportunity for you to begin to discover who you really are. As a tool for this discovery, you will use physical space (your nest) to reveal who you actually consider yourself to be. Your surrounding physical space reflects to yourself and others who you really are.

In the final chapter of Part II, chapter eight, you intentionally design a physical space to reflect who you could be if you were totally unlimited. This is an exciting chapter about using the power of space to create a sustainable future for yourself and others.

CHAPTER 4

The Phoenix Effect—
From Ashes to Aliveness

The bird proudly willing to burn,
So that he may live again,
Chooses the flames of fires
That burn the aged Phoenix
The nature stands still
Till a new young bird starts again,
and begins the legend of the Phoenix.

— Claudius Claudianus (Claudian), Roman author

IN CHAPTER 3, you were given the first part of the code associated with the Phoenix Myth. It's to assume the point of view that the Phoenix is in essence you, then say, "This story is about me. I am a Phoenix." Look at the Phoenix Myth through this point of view, find in it the connections, correlations, and clues about your life.

The next part of the code is the Phoenix Effect. The Phoenix can reinvent itself in the face of a major breakdown; so can you. It is possible for you to use the Phoenix Effect to deal with aging. In this chapter, we examine in detail what that looks like.

The First Stage of the Phoenix Effect: A Severe Disruption to Life as Usual

In life, it usually takes a tragedy or external life-wrenching circumstance to blast us loose from our normal, common, everyday way of being. When such happens, we draw on our unrecognized yet inherent power to newly invent our lives. I call the expression of the renewal of possibility the Phoenix Effect. The Phoenix Effect is best created in life when life is the way you don't want it to be.

Together my wife Mary Louise and I experienced a profound example of such a life-wrenching event that caused us to experience the Phoenix Effect. As you read about what happened to us, think about a time in your own life when you were plunged into horrible circumstances but discovered a new life of renewal and expansion, rising well beyond your previous limits.

Go back with me to Mother's Day 1988. We are visiting friends to see their new home, and neighbors have gathered for a welcoming barbecue. Our nineteen-month-old son Adam toddles into the new house with Mary Louise as our friends show her their new home; because they have not yet moved in, the house is empty.

Mary Louise holds Adam's hand while they are going upstairs. As they walk down a hall, Adam pulls away from her and starts running after our friends' children, who are five and seven. Mary Louise is unconcerned; since the house is empty, there is nothing to climb on or get into. As she enters a room, talking to her friend, Mary Louise sees Adam reaching out to touch the screen of a ceiling-to-floor window. The unlatched screen gives way under his touch and he disappears from sight through the second-story window.

It is the beginning of a Phoenix event in our lives.

Mary Louise takes a step toward the window, even though Adam is already gone. The room seems to turn into a long, dark tunnel. As she remembers that moment, she realizes that she suffered a severe mind shock. She is screaming (though she later recalls that she couldn't scream); I can hear her. She pushes past her friend's husband, who is running up the stairs, probably because he hears her screaming. He grabs hold of her arm and she struggles and frees herself. I yell, "What happened?" She shouts to me, "Adam fell from the upstairs window!"

As Mary Louise bursts through the front doorway, I am already kneeling over our little son on the concrete driveway, checking for a pulse and breath. Adam is sprawled face down on the pavement. As Mary Louise comes outside, he raises his head and begins to cry. As he cries, we both know he is alive—but not knowing how badly he is hurt, we kneel beside him, cradling and soothing him, waiting out the eternity until the ambulance arrives. The paramedics take over, checking and stabilizing. Mary Louise rides to the hospital in the ambulance with Adam while I follow in the car.

At one point in the ambulance, Adam's eyes roll back in his head like he is losing consciousness. Mary Louise calls to him to stay right there with her, to look at her. He comes right back and remains present. After his immediate evaluation and treatment in the emergency room, he is taken for an x-ray. Because Mary Louise is pregnant, I go into the x-ray room with him.

Adam has skull fractures in three places; his mandible joint is also fractured, but that is the smaller threat. They perform a brain scan. Adam is fortunate. The fractures are simple with no indentations, so there is no damage to his brain. The doctor tells me he will have some swelling in his brain from the trauma, but it will resolve itself in about six weeks.

That was the accident that precipitated our Phoenix event—and it also precipitated a difficult time in our marriage. Mary Louise and I dealt with Adam's accident in totally different ways. I was intellectual about it; I figured Adam was going to be okay, so we needed to get over it and get on with it. I threw myself back into my work and got on with life. My work required that I travel all but eight days a month; when I was home, I was on conference calls and preparing for my next assignment. There wasn't a lot of relating going on.

During that time I especially didn't want to deal with how Mary Louise was coping with Adam's accident. She blamed herself, and deep post-traumatic stress took a huge toll on her. I was making her wrong for being so emotional about the accident; she was making me wrong for being so unfeeling about it all. I handled our frightening accident by doing more work; she handled it by overprotecting Adam as she suffered severe stress.

She later told me that she felt so alone and angry because it seemed I wasn't there for her. Instead of listening to her and just expressing understanding and offering comfort, I tried to *fix* her so she would just "get over it." I got angry and impatient with her when I considered her to be too emotional. We later learned that this is not at all unusual for a husband and wife whose child is seriously injured or killed. Statistically, about 75 percent of these couples get divorced.

The week Adam came home from the hospital, Mary Louise miscarried; I was out of town. A friend came over to stay with Adam, and Mary Louise had to drive herself to the hospital. She had to have a dilation and curettage (D&C), a surgical procedure to prevent infection after a miscarriage. The hormonal shift of losing a pregnancy combined with the emotional trauma of witnessing the near death of Adam and the loss of our unborn child to wreak even more havoc on her already out-of-control emotions. She literally cried most of her waking hours.

The only thing that held her together was the responsibility of taking care of Adam. In the days following his accident, Adam began to have some petit mal seizures; each one scared Mary Louise to death and sent her running to the hospital. The doctor assured us that such seizures are not too unusual with the inflammation and swelling in the brain in the weeks following a head injury. He also told us to make sure that Adam didn't bump his head. Can you imagine the exhaustion involved in following a toddler around all day to make sure he doesn't bump his head?

After the miscarriage, the burden of Adam's care certainly fell mostly on Mary Louise; I was out earning a living. We will ever be so grateful for the ladies from our church. They really exemplified Christian charity. The women came in four-hour shifts while Mary Louise was recovering from her miscarriage; they cleaned our house, cooked for us, and even ironed my shirts. And they took turns shadowing Adam, the energetic toddler.

At the time of his accident, Adam was nineteen months old and his speech was very advanced for his age. After the accident, he didn't talk at all for about three months. He dragged his right leg in an awkward gait. Mary Louise was worried and anxious about him all the time. In addition to frequent neurological testing, he underwent regular physical and speech therapy for about six months. It was such a hard time. As I reflect back on this, I don't know how people deal with injuries and illnesses where there is no hope of getting better. Mary Louise is actually pretty sturdy and handled it like a trooper, but her hormones were so unbalanced and erratic after the miscarriage that she stayed angry at me for not being there. From my perspective, I had stayed focused on my work to provide for us.

At the time of Adam's accident, Mary Louise was working on a master's degree in psychology and counseling. After his accident and her miscarriage, she was so emotionally distraught that she couldn't concentrate on her reading and other work. It took her an hour to read a page, and when she got to the end of a paragraph, she realized that she had no idea what she had just read. Where she had previously been very efficient and multi-task-oriented, she couldn't cook a meal and have everything done at the same time. It took her forever to clean the house. She'd burst into tears just driving down the road. Eventually she had to give up working on her graduate degree in psychology.

Mary Louise started having fearful imaginings. As she washed the dishes, she imagined someone might drive by and shoot at us through the window. If she took Adam to the park in the stroller, she imagined that a car would jump the curb and hit them. Her feelings were classic symptoms of Post-Traumatic Stress Disorder (PTSD), something that doesn't just go away. We decided to seek counseling for her and found a therapist who specialized in PTSD. After just a few weeks of counseling, she was getting a grip back on her life; the symptoms started receding.

The Second Stage of the Phoenix Effect: Rising Out of the Ashes into a New Life

It was during this time of recovery from Adam's accident that Mary Louise noticed an ad in the Sunday newspaper for a school of Taekwondo, a martial art that originated in Korea. Now the national sport of Korea, its rules and vocabulary are established by the government of Korea. It involves very precise patterns of kicking and punching and usually includes full-contact sparring. Taekwondo is now an Olympic sport.

The ad claimed that Taekwondo could improve physical fitness, mental focus, and self-confidence. That claim spoke to her. After four miscarriages and the birth of Adam, she was in the worst physical shape of her entire life. She was twenty-five pounds overweight and couldn't even run a block. She also would have described herself as handicapped in the area of mental focus. And her self-confidence had been shattered—after all, she judged that she couldn't even keep her own child safe.

Mary Louise wanted to try Taekwondo in an attempt to recover her health and well-being. She knew she needed exercise, and Taekwondo looked to her like it would be more fun than the common exercises like running, walking, swimming, and weight lifting.

She followed up on the ad the next day. When she walked through the door of Master William Kim's Family Taekwondo Training Center in Vallejo, California, she couldn't imagine what he must have thought when he found out she was inquiring for herself and not for her child. Actually, I'll be eternally grateful to Master Kim for not treating her like a middle-aged woman who must be nuts for wanting to learn Taekwondo at her age. He treated her like any other student and expected her to do what every other student did. She said she felt like a beached whale while all the teenage students in the class seemed like agile dolphins. She felt ridiculous when she first tried to do the techniques. She would come home and hardly be able to walk up or down the stairs because she was so sore. She would sleep in a bathtub filled with hot water, trying to ease the pain. It's a wonder she didn't drown!

I can't imagine why she kept going through all the frustration, feelings of inadequacy, and horrendous muscle soreness. One adult told her he had tried Taekwondo for about a month but that it was too much for him. He didn't think an adult could be flexible enough or have the balance, strength, or endurance that Taekwondo required—much less deal with the muscle stress and strain at a mature age. His opinion was that Taekwondo was just for kids. He's a perfect example of the fact that anyone can say anything; the problem is that people think what they say is real. He quit after six weeks. He encouraged her to give it up too. She was ten years older than he was, and he was certain she wouldn't be able to continue. That might have had something to do with why she kept going.

Instead of quitting, she got stronger and started dropping weight. Her mood changed from depressed and fixated on Adam's accident to being more engaged in life, more focused, and more alive. Even so, I never would have believed at that time that she would compete at a world-class level in full-contact Taekwondo, train with the U.S.

Olympic team, become a sixth-degree Black Belt Master Instructor, and become an International Referee in the sport—but that's exactly what she did. Like the Phoenix, Mary Louise was rising newly from the ashes of her past and present life.

After six months of training in Taekwondo, her symptoms of PTSD disappeared completely. Her counselor had told her that the normal course of therapy for PTSD would be about two years, and that she could expect her symptoms to slowly diminish over that period of time until they completely disappeared. That PTSD specialist became so interested in Mary Louise's accelerated progress that she began recommending Taekwondo to all of her PTSD patients. The therapist theorized that the cross-patterning associated with Taekwondo developed new neuropathways in the brain for focus and concentration, two of the most significant deficiencies associated with PTSD. She also theorized that children with attention deficit disorder would improve by practicing Taekwondo. Mary Louise has subsequently proved that theory to be correct for the students in her own martial arts school.

The therapist also thought that the self-defense aspect of Taekwondo builds new self-confidence—and it is important that we **complete** our issues, situations, and attachments if we are ever to be free to have a new life. Experiencing how fragile life is through an accident often shatters the illusion of our safe continuation of life. In other words, we naturally expect to keep living comfortably and as we always have. Accidents show us that we, or those we love, can be snuffed out at any moment. The illusion of safety is shattered. Life is dangerous. When a person becomes skilled in the martial arts, he or she becomes stronger in the face of the risk of life and grows in self-confidence.

Taking on an athletic game like martial arts is a fertile practice for developing self-confidence. Engaging in a full-contact sport also generates courage. It demands that you be fully present. If you are older, you can engage in a non-contact sport, but if you do a full-contact one, you will have to be awake or you'll have a fist or a foot in your face. Pain is sometimes a good teacher. In PTSD, lack of focus is the person's way of not wanting to be present to the danger and pain that life can deal us. We don't want to be aware of that. We are trying to avoid looking at the truth of that. Taekwondo demanded that Mary Louise be present again. It was like someone threw her a life preserver when she had been drowning. Taekwondo brought her back to life. But remember—She *chose* to return to life!

That was Mary Louise's journey out of the ashes. As for me, Adam's accident crystallized my unwillingness to experience emotion—both mine and that of others. Like many men, I had always stuffed my feelings and carried on like it was no big deal. I thought I communicated well and knew myself, when in fact I didn't have a clue as to what real communication was. I had become complacent about listening. In this very difficult time of our lives, I actually

Mary Louise ageless and alive at 65!

learned that the most important aspect of communication is listening—really getting and understanding another person's world from their communication. Before this time, I had no idea what I was feeling; it was like I was living only on the surface of life, never looking at the immense swirl of emotion underneath. Even though my upbringing didn't provide a good model for a satisfying marriage relationship, I wanted to learn to listen with compassion and empathy. I began communicating and really listening, allowing Mary Louise to go through whatever she was feeling without judging her, discounting her, or trying to fix her.

Together, Adam's accident and my cancer changed the way I feel and communicate. I have had to learn to be aware of my own feelings and to communicate them in a straightforward way. Even when I don't want to sympathize with the feelings of others, I now better understand exactly how they are and what they are feeling. I am committed to filling Mary Louise's needs, and I have had to learn how to listen, how to let her know that I understand and appreciate how she feels, and how to understand what she has to deal with on a daily basis.

In effect, then, Adam's accident caused me to rise up into a new world of sensitivity and support for others. A transformation was taking place for me, for Mary Louise, and for our marriage relationship. Of course, like all of us, I am still learning!

As our Phoenix Effect kicked in and I began to listen, Mary Louise was able to move through her emotions and start to heal on her own faster. I learned that when real communication is present, so are love and affinity.

True communication is about being with the other person including hearing what they are saying instead of merely judging, evaluating, and reacting to what we think is being said. True communication also includes being able to get how it is in another person's world. As you are engaged in cracking the Phoenix Myth, look for the messages and practices that can lead you into more effective connection with others.

We got through our son's accident without getting divorced. We pulled the statistics a little in the other direction.

The Third Stage of the Phoenix Effect: Rising Up Again Beyond the Best of the Past

As she continued her training, Mary Louise won a U.S. National Championship then a World Championship—all gold in Taekwondo. She went on to win the U.S. Nationals twenty-one times and the annual World Championship nine times in full-contact competition. This extraordinary self-expression of life was not likely to ever happen for her without the Phoenix Effect.

Some of Mary Louise's World Championship medals, earned while in her fifties. These demonstrate the kind of unpredictable results obtained from the Phoenix Effect.

Here's the message for you in all of this: With confidence in the Phoenix Effect, you can say yes to things that look impossible. In any circumstance and at any age, you can choose to experience life newly. Mary Louise's Phoenix Effect has endured and expanded for nearly twenty-five years—the Phoenix Effect and your reinvented life are sustainable.

When you create your Phoenix Effect, using the Seven Keys that we'll soon explore in detail, you will just keep playing your new life game—regardless of how it looks, regardless of what you think is possible or what everyone else thinks is possible—because you are being who you never were. You can create an unpredictable future that gives you an extraordinary now.

All humanity advances when a human being interacts with life as if the impossible were possible and then perseveres until it is. You make a powerful difference when you shatter your perceived limits and **sing your unique song**. While living the Phoenix Effect you discover at a deeper level that unique song and the immortal aspect of you.

Our first Phoenix Effect experience taught us both an incredible life lesson. Now in her late sixties and still competing internationally, Mary Louise has clearly demonstrated that we can use life's dreaded catastrophes and circumstances to invent ourselves newly, **choosing** to create the possibility of living life fully regardless of our age. She and others have shown that it's possible to build on the momentary wreckage a new and glorious life beyond the predictable, normal, day-to-day drift of things.

Since that first experience, we discovered that you and I are not limited to one Phoenix Effect. If you think about it, you'll likely discover that you have already had one or more such occasions when, Phoenix-like, you have risen from pain, deadness, and damaging low points of your life. In this odyssey, you will delve deeper into the Phoenix mystery and unlock the secrets of dealing powerfully with aging as one of those predictable low points from which you will rise triumphant.

Actions

Complete the following. Use your Phoenix journal to capture your notes and insights.

1. List three examples of Phoenix Effect experiences from your life or another person's.

2. When in life did you take on a new game and transform your normal way of being? Describe it.

3. Looking at the lives of famous people, find examples of rising from the ashes into a glorious new existence. List five.

4. List three examples of groups that have experienced a Phoenix Effect. An example I can think of is the Oakland Athletics Baseball team.

CHAPTER 5

Choose Your Ageless Life Now!

If I don't manage to fly someone else will.
The Spirit wants only that there be flying.
As for who happens to do it,
He has only a passing interest.
— Ranier Maria Rilke

N ow you know what the Phoenix Effect is. So how do you apply it to aging?

It all begins with **choosing**.

The Phoenix was getting older. It may have been a hundred years old, five hundred years old, or five thousand years old, depending on which version of the myth you are reading. But regardless of its age, it was tired and old.

Like most creatures that get older—including us—the Phoenix could have done nothing. You know what that looks like: being resigned, putting up with, tolerating, adapting, and making all the more comfortable moves to avoid the risk of saying "I will do this, and I will not fail." It looks like living life day by day at a petty pace.

But that's not what the Phoenix did. Instead, there was a moment in time when the Phoenix made a choice: "I will end this old and frail existence. I will take charge and recover my youthfulness."

A choice begins with speaking the choice into existence. It is not based on predictability. A prediction sounds something like this: "I am on the right path, and I can see that if I do more of the same, things will turn out." That's not what happened to the Phoenix. The Phoenix may not have known at all how this adventure in becoming ageless would turn out—but at a precise moment, the Phoenix declared that things would be different.

Have you ever noticed how difficult it is to change yourself? How many times do we really succeed in keeping New Year's resolutions? How many times do we commit to the simplest things in life, exercising regularly, or losing weight and then go back to business as usual within a week? How many times do we take a self-development program but don't internalize suggested new ways of being? Most of us have a library of impotent notebooks from the courses we've taken—and they amount to nothing more than a wish and a want!

Breakthroughs never happen in the domain of playing it safe and staying the same, yet for the most part that is how human beings appear to be designed. Staying the same preserves the limited view you have of yourself and maintains the myth of Me. You become a noun rather than a verb; you are fixed rather than flying! What is it you don't know that you don't know about yourself? How are you limited by being a human being?

The first part of the Phoenix Code says: This myth illuminates your real nature. *You* are the Phoenix discussed in the myth. That means you are a chooser, and you can choose—you can commit to your choice and keep your word. You can choose, keep your choice alive, and stay focused on it. You can choose the impossible game of interrupting how you are currently aging and will predictably continue to age.

You can:

- Accept the risk of your choice.
- Create an audacious vision of getting biologically younger.
- Cause lower blood pressure, lower blood sugar, and improved biomarkers that indicate your health.
- Give yourself a new mindset about who you are and the power you have in life.
- Begin to use technology to positively impact your well-being and energy.
- Focus attentively on what it takes to be ageless.
- Play this ageless game full out.

That's what the Phoenix did. It chose and committed. It didn't know how to do what it wanted, so in some versions of the myth it began with a prayer to Ra (the sun god) to make itself younger. The Phoenix did not receive an answer, so in most versions of the myth the Phoenix decides to fly away from Arabia, where it had been living, and to be complete with its past life.

The First Key: Choose and Commit to a New Life of Ageless Instead of Aging

The first of the Seven Keys: Choose and commit to succeed. You are choosing a new life of being ageless instead of the drift of a life of predictable aging. Now lets look at commitment in more detail. Abraham Lincoln did a great job in summing up commitment when he said:

Commitment is what transforms a promise into reality.

It is the words that speak boldly of your intentions and actions that speak louder than the words.

It is making time when there is none. Coming through time after time, year after year.

Commitment is the stuff character is made of; the power to change the face of things.

It is the daily triumph of integrity over skepticism.

Here is your opportunity to **choose** having the rest of your life be the best of your life! Here is a form you can use to remind yourself of your choice:

My Choice

    I, _____, commit to do the work to create a future that exceeds my past. I will pay the price required to design and bring forth my life's dreams and take the actions to live a life of full self-expression.

I understand that the goals, dreams, visions, and action plans of my life can be transformed as I complete this book and as I commit to this transformation.

I pledge to myself to successfully live my life fully beginning at whatever age I am now.

_____   _____

Signature   Date

Given your choice above, you are now the chooser. The game in life is to choose to own your power to create new ways of being, and like the Phoenix, come forth anew. Choosing a new perspective regarding who you are, and **being** "I am that" allows for your new life to naturally emerge.

Actions

Complete the following. Use your Phoenix journal to capture your notes and insights.

1. Take the point of view that the Phoenix Myth is about you. List five new characteristics that you can now see about yourself. For example, the Phoenix is immortal, which would make you immortal.

2. What is the first key of the Phoenix Myth that you can use to live an ageless life?

3. Are you committed to living an ageless life? What would your life look like if you were to take sustainable action to do that?

CHAPTER 6

Leaving 'Me' and Entering the World of the Phoenix

The more space and emptiness you can create in yourself,
then you can let the rest of the world come in and fill you up.
— Jeff Bridges

T O TRAVEL TO THE WORLD OF AGELESS LIVING, you must discover where you are now. Simply put, you are stuck in an unquestioned view of yourself that I call the **myth of Me**. I'll show you how to dismantle that myth so you can break out of it and go looking for **you**.

Mary Louise's Phoenix Effect transformation stimulated an expansion of my life's work that illuminates aging and living an ageless life. I have traveled to many countries and have trained and coached about three hundred thousand people from various cultures and countries during the last forty years. My work has primarily been about exploring the humanness we all share—exploring ways we are all the same. Normally, we each are focused automatically on how we differ from one another. Although there is a vast reservoir of a human commonality that impacts each of us profoundly, we mostly ignore our similarities. We can ignore that commonality all we want but it still runs our life.

Start to notice how we as humans focus mainly on our differences. Aren't most of our wars about our differences? Politicians and national leaders often use **the enemy** and fear of the enemy in an attempt to unite as well as control people. But think about aliens: When they invade the planet, I'm sure we will finally be united as the humans versus the aliens! That's a recurring theme of science fiction—in the face of a common external enemy, all human kind will discover we are already one at a very deep level.

So how would an alien describe human beings to other aliens on her home planet? If we could see ourselves from outside ourselves, what would we see as our commonality? Do all humans want to be loved? Are there common thoughts we all think? At the core are we good or bad? Does good or bad depend on who is describing good or bad—and what determines that point of view?

Life has a main agenda for you and me: It's called *survival*. The neurological wiring of the brain keeps us the same so we can avoid the risks of our existence. That ensures survival. It's not limited to survival of the physical body. It includes survival of our beliefs, our points of view, our attitudes, our ways of being, our mental states, our feelings and emotions, our opinions, our judgments, our political viewpoints, and our imaginary limits we believe about ourselves and that we so stubbornly cling to. It includes survival of all you are right now.

It also includes survival of the myth of Me! Here's how it works: We say, "I'm this way; I'm not that way. I'm good; I'm not bad. I'm an atheist, I'm a Muslim, I'm a Christian. I'm an American." It's a myth! Life is like a stage, and we each play our part—the problem is, we play the same part over and over and over. Somehow we forget we are the actor or actress and we are stuck in a role that is mainly a result of our circumstances. It's a role "full of sound and fury—signifying nothing" (Shakespeare).

After you have lost your true self, all you have left is the role—the myth of Me. The American playwright, Eugene O'Neil, said it very powerfully:

> None of us can help the things life has done to us. They're done before you realize it, and once they're done they make you do other things until at last everything comes between you and what you'd like to be, and you've lost your true self forever.
>
> —Eugene O'Neill, *Long Day's Journey Into Night*

You are stuck in playing who you think you are—a thing designed to stay the same, always recognizable, with only very minor changes allowed. Sometimes, very seldom, you escape and are in the flow. These times are known as peak experiences. Haven't you noticed how difficult it is to change yourself or get out of the box?

You're not actually **any-thing**! For thousands of years, human beings have unquestionably accepted the assessment of previous generations that we are no more than any other thing in the physical world—a myth. You look like something because your body is found in space and exists in time as all things in this world do. But you are more than your body. Who you are is so much more than an aging piece of meat. Who you really are includes being an unchangeable observer of the body. In your brain's automatic attempt to stay consistent and maintain a recognizable you, you use others' and your own description of yourself to maintain the illusion or myth of Me.

Consider that you may be no-thing. If you can get this, you will start to claim a power to reinvent yourself. Like the Phoenix, you can leave the past behind and rise from the ashes of the myth of Me to the freedom to create and bring forth a new and glorious self over and over as time goes on. When you are no longer stuck in "thing-ness," you will also be in touch with being ageless.

What you think, what you believe, what you feel is commonly regarded by you as real. We will fight to the death for what we personally or collectively consider to be important. What is that? To get your hands on the ageless life, you have to see where your foot is nailed to the floor before you can begin to move forward.

To repeat, who are you really? Are you really who you think you are? (I'm not singling you out—I'm referring to all of us.) By engaging in an uncommonly intense inquiry into who you are, perhaps you can loosen the grip of unexamined limiting assumptions about yourself—the myth of Me—and gain access to inventing a way of living beyond ordinary, experiencing life newly, and discover yourself in a new life, just like the Phoenix did.

People often say, "I am who I am." While that may be technically accurate, it doesn't necessarily mean that we know who we are. With very few exceptions, I assert that we don't really know who we are individually, nor do we know who we are as human beings. What we do have are world views and mindsets that define, to us, who we are. But those world views and mindsets are not reality. *How can you sing your unique song if you don't know who you are?*

The myth of the Phoenix provides allegorical references to who we really are. We certainly are so much more than a skin bag or a thing. We generally relate to ourselves and each other as if we are the thing known as our body. In that paradigm, the automatic decline of aging is very predictable and inevitable. It involves a thing—the body—getting older. But if you use the Phoenix Code and assume you are a Phoenix, you see life through the lens of being a Phoenix. Then you are no longer a thing, but an immortal Being.

I know you have some ideas and thoughts about who you really are, but are you willing to look newly at who you are? Are you willing to be in wonder about you and your existence and discover yourself?

Like a Phoenix, you are unique—one of a kind. But your uniqueness is shaped and restricted by being a human being. Your individuality occurs inside the limiting box of human being. The all-pervasive culture of human being in which you exist intrinsically determines most of who you can be—it is your natural or physical nature. So what are we as human beings?

Some of the greatest philosophical, spiritual, and scientific minds of all time have pondered the fathomless question, "Who are we?" Let's hear from a few recent ones.

Albert Einstein said it this way:

A human being is part of a whole, called by us, the Universe, a part limited in time and space. He experiences himself, his thoughts and feelings, as something separated from the rest—a kind of optical delusion of his consciousness. This delusion is a kind of prison for us, restricting us to our personal desires and to affection for a few persons nearest us. Our task must be to free ourselves from this prison by widening our circles of compassion to embrace all living creatures and the whole of nature in its beauty.

In 1974, I visited the ashram of Sri Aurobindo, an Indian master who set out to discover what it would take for human beings of all different religions, races, and countries to live together in peace and harmony. Patterning himself after Noah, who gathered every species of animal, Aurobindo and his partner, an Algerian woman known as The Mother, gathered various people from fifty different countries and in 1968 created Auroville, a town outside of Pondicherry on the east coast of India. It is a community with a vision of human unity and youthfulness at any age.

I made the long journey to Auroville because I especially wanted to observe the Auroville School while studying for my doctorate in education. During my visit I saw surprising examples of the most effective teaching methods and practices I'd ever witnessed. Instruction was so engaging that the young people, ranging in age from five to eighteen, actually begged to attend school six days a week. At the end of their very long days, they usually didn't want to go home. They loved learning! I thought about the students in the school where I worked—most were waiting for the bell to ring so they could stampede out of their classrooms at the end of the day.

Education in Auroville involved experiential learning. For example, students built a model of the Alps out of cement and slid down Hannibal's route over the mountains on their bums. But most important, the context of education was not the same at the Auroville school.

In our Western educational systems, memorization of information masquerades as learning. In our schools, we assume that the student has an empty mind and we simply have to put the right data in and they have to reproduce it.

Beyond basic learning skills—such as reading, writing, and arithmetic—that kind of education is seldom sustainable and it doesn't expand or transform the future of that student. In Auroville, the teacher treated the students as gods who already knew all. Their teaching consisted of reminding students to remember. What a difference that mindset made!

With that in mind, here's what Sri Aurobindo believed about us as human beings:

> Behind the appearances of the universe there is the Reality of a Being and Consciousness, a Self of all things, one and eternal. All beings are united in that One Self and Spirit but divided by a certain separativity of consciousness, an ignorance of their true Self and Reality in the mind, life and body. It is possible by a certain psychological discipline to remove this veil of separative consciousness and become aware of the true Self, the Divinity within us all.

Notice how similar Aurobindo's answer was to Einstein's description. One was an Eastern master, the other a Western scientist. But these two great teachers, who come from totally different cultures, essentially said the same thing in slightly different words.

Now consider the teachings of Bhagavan Sri Ramana Maharshi, another enlightened master from India, in comparison to the Phoenix Myth. As you read, keep speculating on who you might really be if you were not who you think you are:

> Bhagavan Sri Ramana Maharshi's fundamental teaching was that we are the Deathless Spirit, eternal, free, never born, and never dying, which is why we do not truly believe we are going to die, even in the midst of death of the physical body.

In my opinion, what Maharshi is saying is that we are deathless; in the myth, the Phoenix is being an immortal being. You have seen that a major element to understand the Phoenix Code is the assumption that you and I are the Phoenix. This myth is about us! That would mean that consistent with this interpretation we are immortal! In addition, consider this:

> Maharshi taught that perfect unending happiness is our real nature; this alone is the reason why we yearn for it above all. Our tendency though, is to seek happiness in the external physical world, through the mind and the senses, which is a similar confusion as thinking that who we are is our physical body. Sensual pleasure, he said, is the counterfeit form of true spiritual joy. He taught that desire is the source of misery, which is why those who lack attachment to the physical are the happiest. Attachment is the key word. Maharshi taught that all manifested life

is ruled by the law of Karma, the law of cause and effect, known generally as the law of retribution, but is also the law of reward. In other words, we reap the rewards or pay the penalties appropriate to our every act in this life and all prior or successive lives. He says that this connection to ongoing lives is why evil sometimes seems to be rewarded and good punished.

For eight years I studied Yoga rather intensely, meditating for hours daily. I pursued the teaching of Paramahansa Yogananda, the first Yogi to move to the United States from India. He came for the purpose of teaching Americans ancient Indian spiritual views of reality, the truth of our being, and the path to our greatness through self-realization. Read the summary below of some of his teachings; notice how they relate to your view of existence and reality.

Yogananda taught that the entire universe is God's cosmic motion picture and that individuals are merely actors in the divine play; we each change our roles through reincarnation (dying and being reborn in a new body). He taught that harm befalling a seemingly innocent person is the result of karma from a past life. But he advised us not to take this divine delusion any more seriously than we would a movie or television show. He taught that mankind's deep suffering is rooted in the error of identifying too closely with one's current role rather than identifying with the movie's director, or God.

He also said, "World is a large term, so a man must enlarge his allegiance, considering himself in the light of being a world citizen. A person who truly feels the world is my homeland—it is my America, my India, my Philippines, my England, my Africa—will never lack the scope for a useful and happy life. His natural local pride will know limitless expansion; he will be in touch with creative universal currents."

In light of what these masters, sages, and scientists have said, we can now innovatively consider who we really are. I suggest that the Phoenix Myth will point at both who you are and who we all collectively are!

Ask yourself this question: Is the I that I think I am who I really am? Is it only an illusion or a creation of my mind? It's a question that requires some thought; read this question several times and don't be in a hurry to answer it.

Most humans consider that they really are who they think they are, who they believe they are, and who they feel they are. They cling to that illusion as if their survival depends on it. Neuroscience has now identified how this mechanism works automatically in our brain. Regarding our interpretations of I or Me according to neuroscientists, the brain sustains this forged and artificial Me, leaving you completely defined by a concept of yourself.

To say this in a slightly different way, we all have our own individualized ways of being that we are convinced are our only ways of being—and we are neurologically wired and automatically confined to live our life within those limits. These limits perpetuate the familiar view of ourselves.

Why is it so hard to change yourself? Just reading affirmations and the latest self-help book rarely produces any lasting change because the thing called Me hasn't disappeared. Me is still around no matter what, and Me is keeping the lid on through all the talk and pretense about change. Me is interested in the minimum amount of change.

Want a perfect example? Studies show that people who win the lottery usually spend or lose the money very quickly if they are not used to having money. Their brains automatically take them back to familiar territory. We are wired to stay the same. We are wired to remain in the same delusions about ourselves no matter what. Thermostats appear to have been set in the major areas of our life.

Here's what it means: You (and all the rest of us) are inextricably attached to your normal way of being. Your brain is addicted to Me—more exactly, to a myth of Me. You have become trapped in your well-known patterns or habitual ways of being. You live life in the box, in the pretense of knowing who you are. The joke is that in reality you are not limited to any one way of being—yet you are living in the all-pervasive illusion of being limited and separate. We are like prisoners who stay in our cells even when the doors are open. We are like the occupants of Plato's cave who prefer the shadows to the frightening light of the world.

The Seven Keys of the Phoenix myth include the Key of Completion. Begin by completing the habit of Me, with all your habitual ways of being, doing, and having. From the ashes you can create the possibility of a magnificent new Me with an unpredictable, unprecedented, glorious future of new adventure and connectedness. You will finally be able to determine who you will be rather than continue living the myth of who you have been believing you are.

Subtle, invisible, and seemingly real, the illusions we believe are the stuff from which we create the world in which we live.

This same principle applies to human aging. We create our ongoing World of Aging from aging as we have been culturally conditioned to know it. *Most of us accept this normal paradigm of aging as the only game in town.* We don't recognize it as only one of many possible choices in the aging game. Instead, it becomes a societal agreement that allows only for the decline associated with aging and for lost ability to do all that you love to do. That is a poor reward for a life well-lived! What if it is a lie?

Actions

To begin to find yourself, complete the following. Use your Phoenix journal to capture your notes and insights.

1. Continue to research the Phoenix Myth. If it's about you, what does it reveal about who you really are (vs. your current myth of Me)?

2. Work with the first key from the Phoenix Myth, the key of choice, and choose to commit to live an ageless life. Choose to have the rest of your life be the best of your life. What would that look like?

3. Imagine that the ancient and enduring Phoenix Myth is about who you are. Then, like the Phoenix, you are supremely special! You are both another human being and one of a kind! You are immortal. You have a beautiful song—one that only you were meant to sing. You can reinvent yourself and rise again. You are not the story you have become. Imagine and write down a glorious future for yourself. Read it every day for seven days.

4. Ask yourself, how can I get out the trap of my self-fulfilling, limiting mindset of feelings, thoughts, and emotions (Me)?

CHAPTER 7

The Phoenix Nest, Your Nest, and Discovering Your Real Self

Our deepest fear is not that we are inadequate.
Our deepest fear is that we are powerful beyond measure.
It is our light, not our darkness that most frightens us.
We ask ourselves, who am I to be brilliant, gorgeous,
talented, fabulous? Actually, who are you not to be?
You are a child of God. Your playing small does not
serve the world.

— Marianne Williamson

WHEN ASKED WHAT THEY ARE, most people would say they're a human being. We know a lot about human, but not much about being ... and this kind of label might have very little to do with who you really are.

To find out who you really are, let's start by considering the scientific explanation of what a human being is—and that includes you. Try this on for size:

You're a pattern of intelligent energy beamed into a water vessel we call the body. Your body is actually a complex hydraulic system that nourishes and transports an unbelievably complex three-pound gem—your brain, the venue for experience. Part of your brain carries out intellectual functions, making you a being with a mind.

You also have a powerful non-conscious dimension that controls not only the autonomic physical functions of your body, but also controls how you interact with life. A potent issue you'll want to eventually consider is how you might go about altering the habitual way in which you interact with life.

As a human being, your brain has a powerful "search engine" called the reticular activation system. You also have a psycho-cybernetic mechanism that regulates every part of your life—things like finances, health, love, and success. Once a set point is established in any domain, your system works doggedly to maintain that setting—after all, it believes that's what you need to survive. You then recognize yourself as being this way. You become comfortable within your normal range of being, doing, and having. And it is very, very uncomfortable to alter that way of being!

Does this description sound accurate? It's actually derived from a Cartesian Newtonian scientific paradigm that many scientists consider to be an outdated, inaccurate description of what a human being is. As you can see, it interprets a human being as nothing more than a thing reacting to other things.

If you're not a thing, then what are you really?

Forget the description you just read, and consider that as a human being, you have the power to create through language who you are—you can declare with firmness, I am who I say I am. If that's true, you can then own that power and use it to expand life rather than limit it. In reality, you've always created your life exactly this way—you were simply unaware of the source of that creative power. You most likely assumed you were an innocent victim of someone else's creation.

Is it possible to discover who you are by using something other than your mind?

Consider the Phoenix Myth—especially the concepts of completion, the space of nothing, and reinvention. Can you find clues there? Do you recognize anything about the nest of the Phoenix? The nest consists of more than just mud and sticks; it's made with myrrh, cinnamon, and other rare and precious herbs. Why is that significant?

The nest is the physical environment of the Phoenix and is a fundamental element of the code contained in the myth. The nest is a space in which the Phoenix exists. It is a reflection in physicality of who the Phoenix is. The precious herb myrrh represents the healing and serving aspects of the Phoenix. Mentioned in the Bible many times, cinnamon was used as a medicine and for embalming, and is a potent antioxidant that represents health and well-being. A gift fit for kings and gods, cinnamon was once so highly prized that wars were fought over it.

In the stories about the Phoenix, these herbs represent perfection, purification, and transformation—and they are mentioned in virtually all versions of the myth. The nest, then, is the exalted space created by the Phoenix as it prepares to transform itself into the next, more glorious stage of its existence.

What is your *nest*? Take some time to consider this question so that your deeper thoughts emerge.

I suggest that the nest of the Phoenix in your life is represented by your physical environment—your home, your car, your garage, your office. What can you say about your nest? What does your nest say about you? Think about it: All of your physical spaces probably have a common pattern.

The beautiful nest of the Phoenix is like a three dimensional mirror that reflects the existential essence and purpose of the Phoenix. Your nest is also a reflection of you. That's why you can enter someone's home, even if she isn't there, and get a sense of who she is from her environment.

You are profoundly connected to the physical world, yet you're likely unaware or at least unconscious of that intricate and intimate connection. Through closely examining your physical environment, you can get a pretty accurate sense of who you really are at a deeper level than what you presently believe about yourself.

It is a known fact that those who dramatically alter their environment will dramatically alter their lives. In fact, one of the greatest inventors and architects of the twentieth century, Buckminster Fuller was reported to have said "You can't change people, but you can change their environment and people will change."

If you change your environment—your nest—your life will change. In your journey to being ageless, you can use the power of physical space to access and expand who you really are and will be in your second half. By altering and expanding your physical space, you invoke your power to consciously create yourself newly.

The physical space of your environment has a powerful impact—and can help you discover who you are and open new possiblities for reinventing yourself. You can design an ageless life by creating an environment that is aligned with your highest self. Doing so will actually impact your physical body, transforming it at the most elemental level.

When you align, organize, and design your physical environment to be consistant with who you really are, you are using space to generate a new way of being. A new way of being calls forth the actions that will naturally result in unimaginable accomplishment correlated to your changed environment.

Creation is the work of being. When being is the dominant aspect of a human being, the physical body is subject to the power of being. To create is to be fully alive, and aliveness is a fundamental element of the nature of being ageless.

Physicality—A Portal to Being

The movie Stargate portrayed a doorway or a portal in Egypt that opened to another universe. That portal beckoned voyagers into the experience of other worlds.

Imagine a ***Portal to Being***, a Stargate into a new universe of you. This Portal to Being can be discovered in your physical environment. It might be found in your home; it could be your car or any other specific physical object. In fact, you might have more than one Portal to Being found in your treasured inanimate objects that inspire, move, and uplift you.

Let me share an example from my own life. My master's degree is in geology. I love rocks and have loved them all my life. In 2008, I found one of the most extraordinary rocks I have ever seen—a stunning amethyst geode, a huge hollow rock with an amethyst crystalline interior. This geode is a museum-quality mineral specimen measuring more than three feet high and two feet wide and weighing about three hundred pounds. Cut in half, it revealed semiprecious, rich purple amethyst crystals throughout the core of its large cavity. But that's not all: scattered throughout the interior are twelve fist size crystals of snow white calcite with veins of tiny amethyst crystals running through them—a feature that makes the geode extremely rare.

I love this rock! Whenever I take time to look at this geode specimen, magnificently displayed in my home, its exquisite beauty profoundly moves me. It speaks to me of success; I feel honored to have something in my living room so radiant and perfect. It reminds me of my commitment to the extraordinary and to excellence in my life. This geode is perfect and complete; it is missing nothing. It is rock solid and inspires me to endure anything life can throw at me. My geode reflects back to me the experience of being powerfully expressed, bountifully contributing that power and splendor to all in its presence. It leaves me feeling like a king.

My magnificent geode is an example of a Portal to Being. It gives me the opportunity to see more clearly who I really am.

Each of us is intimately connected to certain things we treasure. Begin to discover yourself by selecting some special physical object. Look into your thoughts and feelings about it. As an example, here are the things I most appreciate about my geode—my treasured object:

My Descriptive Thoughts About It (outside of me)	What I Say I Feel (inside of me)
Beautiful	Appreciative
Physically Perfect	Peaceful
Unique	Complete
Precise	Moved
Rich	Wonder
Vibrant	Childlike
Ethereal Colors	Uplifted
Brilliant	Blessed
Regal	Rich & Successful
Complete	Amazed
Diamond-like	Fortunate & Fulfilled
Sparkling	Spiritual

In using my description and feelings, I find I can get a deeper sense of who I am by looking outside of myself at this geode. For example, one of my feelings is a sense of the spiritual when I look at this rock, but the rock is just a rock. So I wouldn't feel this way if there wasn't a spiritual

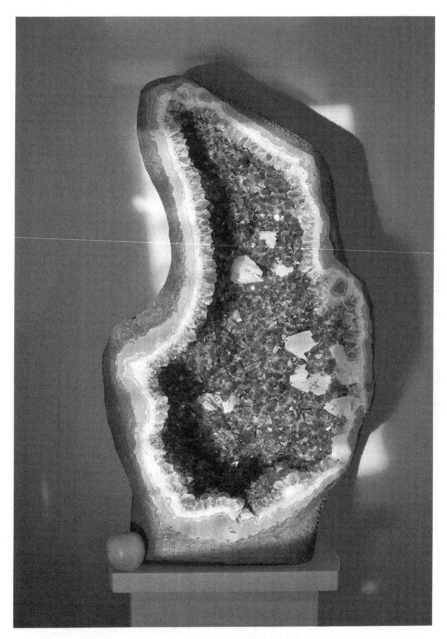

My 300 pound amethyst geode is a remarkable Portal to Being.
It opens an opportunity for discovering the self I really am.

side to me. Also I notice that I describe the rock as perfect, unique, and regal. I suspect that also describes my sense of myself at a deeper level. I couldn't see that in a rock if it wasn't there already in me. My magnificent geode is like a mirror reflecting back to me aspects of myself. This is why I call it a Portal to Being. Your special treasure is an entry into a deeper knowledge of who you really are.

Exercise

To get a clearer picture of who you really are, find an item you treasure. Now identify the actual physical attributes and properties of that item that especially appeal to you. Then list the thoughts and feelings elicited by this item in your Phoenix journal.

You can use your chosen object as your Portal to Being. As such, it can transport you from a false world of what you believe about yourself into a new world in which you discover a deeper level of who you really are.

This treasured object, the Portal to Being you have just identified, is an opening to your true self—a reflection of the real you that exists in the real world. You value this object because it most accurately reveals aspects of your true nature and represents the values that are your very own.

In your Phoenix journal, add this statement to your list: "My Portal to Being reminds me that I am—"

What is your Portal to Being actually made of? Is it made of wood, glass, stone, water, metal, or some combination? If your object is made of mere glass, wood, rock, liquid, or metal, where did all of these values you listed come from?

There are no inherent values in a physical object.

The assigned values and qualities must have come from you, since you are the one who identified them! You found who you are in that physical object—in that Portal to Being. What you value in it is you—the real you looking back at you.

Here's a hint of coming attractions. The more you honor and emphasize those treasured physical objects by dramatically displaying them in your physical environment, the more they reinforce who you really are. Your new environment pulls your unique magnificience into view.

Actions

Answer the following questions and record any new awareness of yourself in your Phoenix journal.

1. What are the five main characteristics of your Portal to Being?

2. How do the characteristics of your Portal to Being show up in your life?

3. Using the special nature of your Portal to Being as a reference to measure from, where in life have you settled for an environment of lower quality?

4. What can you get rid of, clear out, clean up, or organize in your physical environment that will beautify your nest and leave you inspired?

CHAPTER 8

Creating Your Enchanting and Magnificent Phoenix Space

B = f(P, E)
Behavior is a function of the Person and the Environment
— Kurt Lewin

CREATING NEW WAYS OF BEING (new thoughts, new feelings) through recognizing and using the power of the physical space of your environment is truly a new path to transformation.

During the last century, scientists have found that space is a field of endless particles and waves of energy. We can't see them with the naked eye, yet they exist in a state of constant motion and vibration. In other words, everything is energy, including our environment—and including our bodies.

You have seen that your physical environment is intimately connected to your inner space, which relates to your feelings, emotions, and the sense you have of yourself. As a general rule, we as human beings are only superficially aware of our physical environment; mostly we use it unconsciously and decorate it to look good.

Your physical environment can be an existence system for a past-based illusion of who you believe you are. For example, consider how your closet maintains who you were when you selected the clothes that are in it. Your clothes are also a physical expression of who you think you are and what you think you can have. They are the costumes of an actor playing the same part over and over again.

You are empowered to be complete with your past when you become aware of your physical environment. When you intentionally align your environment with your Portal to Being, you bring the rest of your nest to a glorious level. You are creating a self-designed space. Your new physical space reinforces your authentic creative self rather than the reactive and automatic default self of your past. When your authentic self is established solidly in the physical world, it naturally becomes the harbinger of a new future.

When you create beauty, order, design, and function in your nest, a natural flow of workability, creativity, and unpredictable accomplishment occurs aligned with your true self. By taking personal responsibility for your physical space, you can literally generate a new internal space of personal power. You transform yourself.

There is an art to expanding your life by recognizing your real self through your physical space and honoring your environment. While an entire library of books could be written on accessing an ageless and limitless life through your physical space, here are the four basic elements:

1. Clearing out: This develops discernment and exercises choosing.

2. Cleaning: This creates Godliness and clarity.

3. Organizing: This creates flow, function, and quiet order.

4. Designing: This magnifies and glorifies the space.

This four-step process connects and aligns your external world with your internal world, calling forth who you really are.

We read in the book of Genesis that Adam was given the commandment to dress the garden. Consider that owning and being responsible for your physical environment is akin to "dressing the garden." Owning the physical environment requires choosing to be fully conscious of your physical milieu. The action of clearing out, cleaning up, organizing, and designing your physical space brings forth a new degree of consciousness and authentic self-expression. This self-generated space then validates who you really are in the physical world. You have elevated your power!

When you create space, you alter the energy and feeling of a physical environment—and you shape the energy and experience of the people who use it. Consider for example a group that dresses their garden by transforming an old playground into a park. In the process they become connected to each other, creating a community through the space that they personally and collectively created. This process literally brings forth alignment and an experience of closeness. The Amish are masters at creating an experience of community by collectively improving their farms and ranches.

A dirty, disorganized space full of make-do items can create a negative field of energy that represents being powerless and discouraged. You will tend to avoid that space or let it get more cluttered and chaotic. You will most likely feel completely overwhelmed in that space. If your physical space is out of control, I suggest that your life is out of control. If you are disconnected from your physical space, I suggest that you are disconnected from who you really are.

A transformative shift occurs the moment you begin to dress the garden of your personal environment—to clear it out, clean it up impeccably, organize it for function and flow, and design it according to what you really want to have. An environment aligned with who you really are creates a powerful current that carries you into a new future.

Clear out your space! Let go of what you don't need, of what you don't like, and of what doesn't represent the magnificence of you. I don't care if the space is empty and you don't have the money to fill it yet. In the vacuum that you create by rejecting that which is not you, you open up the means to get new precious things that create an environment consistent with who you are. That's part of the Phoenix Effect!

When you clean your space, clean it like you would if Buddha or Jesus were coming to dinner. As you do, you'll notice everything—the dust on the furniture, the marks on the walls, and the repairs that need to be done. You'll see the disorder that goes unnoticed every day—disorder that profoundly impacts you, locks you in the past, and traps you in your false self.

After your space is clear and celestially clean, organize the space to perfectly fulfill the function of that environment. You may further magnify your space by creating beauty as an authentic self-expression. Create a shrine of your Portal to Being and you will know who you are every time you look at it.

Start by reclaiming one area of your environment, then you'll find yourself motivated to reclaim the next. Your physical world will begin to reflect and resonate with who you are. Hopelessness will disappear. You will no longer feel overwhelmed. Your innate self will come forth.

You won't recognize yourself after engaging in this life-changing process. You will have created the space where you can resonate with and be shaped by your true self. Creating your physical space to be an extraordinary environment of order, workability, beauty, and integrity is a springboard into a transformed, authentic, and ageless you. Like the Phoenix, you arise newly!

Taking full responsibility for your physical environment awakens discernment not only in the physical aspect of your life, but in all aspects of life. You not only see what you couldn't see before but also begin to think what you couldn't think before. You begin to be what you have never been before. You feel truly at home in your physical world, as well as having new joy, peace, and satisfaction.

A physical environment that has integrity gives you a sense of unique eloquence, completeness, fluency, and freedom, all of which are vital to your success and happiness. Most people as they get older clutter their nest. Perfecting your nest is one of the biggest secrets to destroying aging and limited living. A perfected nest that is aligned with your true being naturally brings forth an ageless, unlimited life.

Actions

Do the following exercises and record any insights in your Phoenix journal. Choose a space in your environment; if you decide on a shared space, work with those who share the space with you. Use your Portal to Being as a standard by which everything else is measured, and use the following structure to manage your project.

1. In your Phoenix journal, write down the space you decide to transform (for example, your closet, your office, the kitchen, and so on).

2. List what you are going to clear out. By when will you clear it out? If it is a shared space, with whom will you work?

3. What are you going to clean up? By when? If it's a shared space, with whom will you work?

4. What will you organize? By when? And with whom (if you are working with someone)?

5. What will you design? By when? And with whom (if you are working with someone)?

I suggest that you journal and share with others realizations you've gained, victories you've experienced, and breakthroughs you've had. You will have transformed your physical space, creating an alignment where your nest is whole, perfect, and complete.

PART III

Rise from the Myth of Aging with Seven Keys

I N THE NEXT SIX CHAPTERS, we examine in detail the rest of the Seven Keys found in the Phoenix Code. In Part II, we have already considered the first key of the code—to choose. Let me give you an example of how this works in life.

During my two years of dealing with stomach cancer and total immersion into my own survival, I had all of my attention on my body. I stepped back from the commitment I had made in 1976 to stand for the transformation of humankind. The day I chose again to recommit to have the context of my life be about transformation, my whole life distinctly accelerated toward a new aliveness and high performance. Choosing to have my life be about the transformation of life for everyone was clearly one of those lines of demarcation that powerfully impacted the quality of my life.

Choosing is the first key. When you choose to make your life about something bigger than yourself and your personal life, you are using that key. Our chosen context decisively impacts the quality of life, because from that context we invent and live our lives. Choosing a life of service brings fulfillment. Inventing and choosing a context for your life will be the source of unprecedented and expansive self-expression. In my life, when I got cancer, having my own survival be the fundamental context of my life seemed appropriate in order for me to survive, but that context did not expand my self-expression, my sense of purpose, and my fulfillment. I chose to take on empowering the quality of life for all of humanity by teaching communication. This is an example of using the first key—choosing. Without choosing life is mostly reaction or default to our usual way of being.

In terms of aging, as I became immersed in contribution, a strange thing occurred. I forgot about my age and what it meant about what I could or couldn't do. In fact, I noticed that I was seldom concerned with aging or my health. Physical vitality and strengthening became part of the fabric of my life contained in the background. My commitment to empowering people had pushed the health and age concerns aside.

As you use these Seven Keys, you will find you have a new lease on life. In my life, this meant I became renewed and experienced being fully alive and powerful. I even bought a new Harley with my son Ryan. In the past, when we lived near Santa Cruz, California, and Ryan was sixteen years old, we had talked about getting a Harley Davidson motorcycle. This was now a fulfillment of that promise, twenty-three years later.

Striking a blow for ageless with a new Harley.

This was not an old aging persons version of a Harley—this was a big HOG! At first it was very scary for seventy year old me to get on this 750-pound machine and attempt to drive it. Thinking about riding a Harley, looking cool, cruising down the highway is real different from actually riding a Harley. This was new; this was a major challenge. Like a teenager with his first car, I went to a nearby schoolyard after school hours and practiced with Ryan's help. Years later, as I ride the Hog, I am amazed that I didn't give up and give into the normal conversation, "I am too old for this; I could get hurt!"

Be prepared for new forms of self-expression and new adventures as you take on being ageless. I have had some extraordinary rides in some of the most spectacular environments of the U.S., along with my great riding buddies, Mike and Linda Higgins, both world champion power lifters. I would have missed a lot of great times if I had been too old!

As you read about the Seven Keys, look to see how you can apply them in your life.

CHAPTER 9

Completion—Burn Up Your Past and Fly to Freedom

What is to give light must endure burning.
— Viktor E. Frankl

REMINDER: You already have the first key from the Phoenix Myth. What is it? It's choosing: Choose a new future and commit to your choice.

In the Phoenix Myth, the Phoenix chose to be youthful again in the face of the predictable decline of aging. And then it acted to take the journey into a new life—a return to youth. In any way and at any age, we can choose a new future and take action to journey into that new unpredictable future—and commit to bring forth that new future of adventurous, youthful, and ageless living.

The second key is being complete in your life. It involves the critical exercise of completion.

I could have written three books on completing your past. What it boils down to is this: It doesn't take a genius to see that holding onto the past means reliving the past. We relive both the good and the bad, but mostly we relive the "in between." Creating a sustained interruption in the normal flow of your life requires a clearing, or a new space—and unless you clean something out, or complete it, there is no opening in which you can invent and live a new life.

In the Phoenix Myth, the Phoenix prayed for youth and freedom from aging. When it did not receive an answer, the Phoenix began the process of completing its life by flying from Arabia and returning to Egypt. Its intention was to gain access to energy, youthfulness, and new possibilities. When it arrived in Egypt, it gathered twigs of spices and rare herbs and built itself a new nest. The Phoenix then settled into its royal nest, perhaps knowing it was now time to finish letting go of everything it had been. In the myth, its life is completely destroyed by a celestial fire. This created the empty space to bring forth a new life and a new future. It's important to note though that the Phoenix took responsibility for successfully dealing with aging. Instead of waiting around to react to the sun god's intervention, it moved forward toward new youth by flying back to Egypt.

Using this analogy to inspire you to complete your life, look in the various areas of your life where you are stuck—in other words, areas where you are incomplete. As examples, look in the areas of your relationships, career, finances, to name a few. List in your Phoenix journal all the areas where you are incomplete.

What regrets do you have from your past? For example, you might regret that you never finished college. Are you willing to be complete with all your regrets? Are you willing to just forgive yourself and let it all go? What would it take to get them complete? In your Phoenix journal, list all the regrets you still hold.

What resentments do you still have? Who is involved, and what will it take to be complete? For example, you might resent your father for his anger and abuse. Are you willing to forgive and let go of those resentments? In your Phoenix journal, list any resentments you are not complete with.

Do you have any unresolved complaints to which you are attached? What would it take to complete these complaints? List any actions you could take in your Phoenix journal to complete all your complaints.

Are you withholding your acknowledgement or appreciation of anyone? Are you willing to acknowledge that person or people? Make a list in your Phoenix journal of the people from whom you are or have been withholding acknowledgements or appreciation.

What areas of your integrity are incomplete? For example, you might have unpaid traffic tickets, taxes not filed, bills not paid, things borrowed and not returned, or promises not kept, to name a few. List these in your Phoenix journal.

In your Phoenix journal, list the personal characteristics that persist in your myth of Me that keep you incomplete. For example, you might write, "I feel I am always excluded and on the outside looking in." Are you willing to give up (complete) being stuck in these personal characteristics?

Look through all of your incompletion lists and make sure you have listed everything that is currently incomplete. It's critical that the list be thorough. Empting your mind, you will be left with space. This is a very freeing exercise.

When your lists are done, ask yourself, "Is all of this stuff real?" You really think it, say it, do it, and be it—but is it real? Is being incomplete real? Are you really incomplete? Where do these incompletions exist? They only exist in your mind. Of course there are things to complete, but being incomplete exists only in your mind.

What happened before is long gone. The only place it exists is in your listening, thinking, speaking, and experience. It stays around only with you. Who said all that stuff on your lists? Your brain says this stuff, and you listen to it like it is real. It's not real! Your mind comes up with automatic conversations of duality, including the duality of being incomplete or being complete. You may have things to complete, like the payment of old traffic tickets, but you can be complete, even with those tickets unpaid.

When you listen to those automatic conversations of regret or resentment as if they are real, it leaves you constantly feeling incomplete. The access to being complete exists in your power to declare yourself as complete. First, list all of your incompletions; once you can see them rather than try to remember them, set about to complete them. You are the source of completion; you have the power to be complete, and completing things gives you ever expanding power. You can be the angel of completion! It might require communication if you feel incomplete with another person.

You can't really find yourself when you are clouded by the enormity of life's incompletions. On the other hand, when you let go of any of the issues causing you to be incomplete, you will find completeness. Can you just let go of your resentments, regrets, attachments, and so on? Yes; you simply declare them complete and let them go. How do you let go? You choose to let go. Give up your righteousness. Give up your arrogance. Give up thinking your opinions matter at all. You created your resentments and regrets, so while being complete, you can create getting them complete. When you do, you are left with a blank slate necessary for you to create a new future for yourself.

We usually think we have to do something or feel a certain way in order to be complete, but know that you can be complete while you are taking action to complete things in life. Being complete is a declaration: "I am complete. I will resolve what I can resolve. I will communicate with others as necessary. I will do what I can to right the wrongs of my past—and I choose to be complete. People did what they did, things happened the way they happened, and I choose to let it all go. I choose to be complete with every breath of life!"

The Phoenix communicated with the sun god Ra in prayer and supplication. Perhaps communication will play a big part for you in being complete. You can also communicate with people who are no longer living through meditation or in a written letter; you can later burn that letter, offering it up to the universe. Begin the process. Even if you don't experience being complete with each and every issue in your life, you can create a timeless declaration of being complete. You can simply choose to let the incomplete issues go—give them up. Are you willing to be complete? And if so, when?

In life, new experiences and challenging issues always arise. You'll always have things you need to resolve and get complete, but you can deal with them from a perspective of being complete. Incompletions bring feelings of helplessness and hopelessness. The process of completion will create an enormous shift in your life—by specifically defining your incompletions, you can now be responsible for them. You can let them go or take action to complete them, creating new space in your life for whole new worlds of possibility, especially the possibility of life in the World of Ageless Living.

Begin a conscious process of taking action, including having some crucial conversations with people with whom you remain incomplete. Every completion brings you new power. One of the fastest ways to expand your power and overcome helplessness is to complete your incompletions.

When an incompletion comes up again, once again declare it complete. The process is finite; your incompletions won't keep coming up forever. In your new space of being complete, issues of incompletion eventually disappear. You now have space where you can build a new future. Consider this: You may choose to hang on to your incompletions, feeling totally justified about how wronged you were. But going down that path exacts a huge price—your happiness, your peace of mind, and staying stuck in predictably normal aging.

Completing Everything You Have Learned from All of Your Life's Experiences

In his book, *Healthy Aging*, Andrew Weil writes about something he calls ethical wills. In an ethical will, you write a letter about your life to your friends and relatives. Focusing on the lessons learned from all the experiences of your life—good, bad, and everything in between—you write down everything that you have determined to be of value and that you'd like to contribute to others, especially your family and those you love. Writing an ethical will is a great way to get complete with all of your life's experiences.

You can write an ethical will to yourself as well as others as a way to be complete and to leave a legacy about what you have contributed and what you have learned from your life. It's a great way to share your insights, realizations, breakthroughs, and experiences. It also lets you create a new view for yourself of your life: "I have learned what I've needed to learn, and I am complete with everything that has happened to me in my life."

As you write your ethical will, create the experience of being complete with your life. That means everything about your life. Leave no stone unturned. Share what gave rise to the best of you. In the will, be complete about everything in your life to date. Especially share what experiences were the greatest for you that you want others to know about.

To get started, you might begin with something like this: "I wish to leave as my legacy to life and to those I love that which is most precious and of deepest value to me." You could also frame it as a message from you to you: "I am writing to myself in order to review all that I have learned of value and to be complete with all of my life up until to now." Follow by writing everything that happened in your life that would be of enormous value to your family and loved ones. Conclude with something like this: "I declare that with the writing of my ethical will, I am now complete with my life. I leave this discourse as my legacy. I offer it as my personal contribution to life."

I suggest that you stop reading at this point and write your ethical will.

The Mirror Exercise

After you've done the recommended exercises and written your ethical will, you may still feel there are incompletions in your life. If you are addicted to being incomplete, look into a large mirror. With passion and conviction, tell that person in the mirror, "I declare that I am complete with my failures (say each one), recurring problems (say each one), regrets, resentments, self-defeating behaviors, destructive patterns, health issues, career issues, financial issues, relationship issues, emotional issues, irrational behavior issues, mental issues, and spiritual issues. I am complete, because I say I am." Repeat this declaration until the person in the mirror really gets what you're saying. This only works well after you have done the other exercises, including communicating where necessary, and completing your ethical will. This exercise is designed to finalize being complete.

Reminder: The second key to being ageless is completion.

If you do the work described in this chapter, you will be left with lightness and freedom in your life. You don't have to do everything at once, but do the ones right away that you have been putting off and avoiding. This will produce the fastest results.

It's human nature to avoid completing, because we as humans subconsciously try to stay the same. If you don't want to stay the same, completion is essential! Anything incomplete keeps you anchored in the past, while completion cuts your ties to the past and leaves you with a clearing to invent your new future.

Actions

Do the following exercises and record any insights in your Phoenix journal.

1. Review this chapter and make sure you have done all of the exercises to be complete with your past.

2. Share your ethical will with someone you want to be aware of the things you have contributed during your life.

CHAPTER 10

Nothing—The Start of Your Transformation from Aging to Ageless

...something has to die before a new self can be born.
— Gail Sheehan

I WAS IN SYDNEY in the early eighties to lead some training courses in self-development when I asked my assistant, David, "Does Australia have any power spots? You know—a place that is unique, magical, inspiring, regarded as special."

"That would be Ayers Rock, or Uluru," he said. "It's a huge red sandstone monolith twelve hundred feet high and six miles in circumference and features ancient sacred pictographs. It has been a spiritual mecca for aboriginal people for twelve thousand years—maybe longer—making it the oldest church on the planet."

I was intrigued. David continued, "The rock constantly changes colors and appears blood red at sunset. It has great significance to the Anangue people, custodians of the national park that contains Ayers Rock. They claim that a dreamtime track runs right through it."

Ever since I can remember, I have had a reverence for indigenous people and their innate wisdom. Earlier some aboriginals near Sydney had played me a concert on a twenty-five-hundred-year-old didgeridoo and had taken me on a walk-about. I love any opportunity to enter their world. I feel the same way about my work with Native Americans and New Zealand's Maori people.

Since I had to fly from Sydney to Melbourne on that particular trip, I thought I would fly via the northern territories and see this sacred power spot for myself. After all, it was only two thousand miles out of my way!

Days later, I landed at Yulara, a small town about twelve miles from Uluru.

"To the rock, mate?" the tour bus operator asked as I left the small airport. I hesitated; it seemed to me that a quick bus tour wasn't a fitting conclusion to a spiritual journey of thousands of miles. "No thanks," I said, looking around to see where I could buy a canteen. I was excited about the twelve-mile hike across the desert! I was ready for snakes, flies, heat, and whatever else I might find between here and that distant red plateau on the horizon. With nothing but a canteen, a hat, shorts, a t-shirt, and a spirit of wonder, I set out on my personal walk-about.

First there were the flies—and more flies! I encountered more flies in five steps than I had seen in my entire life. They filled my nose and ears and covered my eyes. The only way I avoided suffocation was by constantly waving my hat frantically in front of my face. All the while I had to be on the alert for the snakes—among the most poisonous in the world.

Then there was the heat. As the afternoon progressed, the temperature went above 110 degrees. But as the rock grew larger in my vision and, as promised, started constantly changing colors, I mostly forgot all about the flies, the snakes, and the heat. Well, maybe not about the snakes. This distant, shape-shifting rock created a quieting effect in both my inner and outer worlds.

After four hours of hiking, I finally reached the glowing red giant stone just as the sun was setting. Uluru emerged magnificently from the desert floor. I was completely alone—no tourists, no anyone.

An absolute stillness enveloped me as I explored large canyon-like cracks in the side of Uluru. My usual restless thoughts were replaced by pure awareness and presence. I was home. Never had I so fully transitioned from a thing to a clearing—a space. Freedom washed over me, freedom from ever-noisy thoughts and feelings. It was a pure transforming moment in the void, and I knew I would never be the same. It was a Phoenix moment of seeing myself in the mirror of nothing.

It was getting dark as I climbed the twelve hundred feet to the top of the rock. A few hours later, as I tried to sleep in the howling winds, the spirits of ancient warriors began to make their presence known with cries and screams. Never was the veil between reality and unreality so thin for me. The noise of ancient battles soon made it impossible to sleep, and I spent the strangest night of my life on top of that rock.

The early light of the next day flooded the top of Ayers Rock. I walked over to the edge of a cliff and looked out over the flat desert. It may have been an illusion, but I saw the curvature of the earth as if I were looking at it from outer space. I realized that with nothing present and with being nothing, I could create anything.

I created my rites of passage. I created being a man from that point forward.

I saw significant changes right away as a result of my experience. The next week was filled with extraordinary effectiveness in life and unpredictable results.

I invite you to enter into nothing now—right now, at this point in your life. Create the space for a life that is unlimited, a life of possibility.

What is left when your past is complete? Nothing is left—No-thing is left. This is the third key to the ageless life—the space of nothing, which is also the space of everything. When the Phoenix burns up, there is nothing left. Like the Phoenix, having completed your life, you are left with nothing. There is nowhere to get to and nothing to fix. You are left in the void, in space, nowhere and in no time.

Things normally exist in time and have a location in physical space. But someone really got it wrong about human beings. We are not things.

Don't just read about this; create the experience of nothing. Allow yourself to experience the void. To experience the space of nothing, follow the Phoenix into the void. The following quotes might help you access the world of nothing for yourself.

In *Timon of Athens*, Shakespeare wrote, "Nothing brings me all things."

e.e. cummings wrote this carefully crafted poem about nothing:

what Got him was Noth

ing & nothing's exAct

ly what any

one Living(or some

body Dead

like

even a Poet) could

hardly express what

i Mean is

what knocked him over Wasn't

(for instance) the Knowing your

whole (yes god

damned) life is a Flop or even
to
Feel how
Everything (dreamed
& hoped &
prayed for
months & weeks & days & years
& nights &
forever) is Less Than
Nothing (which would have been
Something) what got him was nothing

St. John of the Cross wrote (translated):

In order to arrive at having pleasure in everything,
Desire pleasure in nothing.
In order to arrive at possessing everything,
Desire to possess nothing.
In order to arrive at being everything,
Desire to be nothing.
In order to arrive at knowing everything,
Desire to know nothing.

The space of nothing is available as an experience. You may deepen your experience of nothing through the power of meditation. The true experience of nothing is also the experience of all things or everything. Said another way, if nothing is present, you are in the space of everything.

According to research done in neuroscience, everything in your awareness is first created in the space of your mind. The commonly accepted world of Newtonian and Cartesian physics is applicable to things and is incongruous with the reality of the being of human being. There is a new world revealed by quantum mechanics and string theory.

Consider that you may be a space, not a thing. Perhaps you are space as in the space of nothing and everything.

The Loss of Nothing—Body Identification

As a space in the space of nothing, how old are you? You don't have an age—you are ageless. Therefore, what you have always thought about aging and you is a lie. It is your physical body that is aging, and you are not merely your body. Believing that you are your body is just as ridiculous as an astronaut believing that she is her space suit. You have a body; you are not just your body!

When you agree with the cultural mindset about aging, you buy into the superstition that you are your body and that you are getting older. When you blindly go along with the all-encompassing lie that you are your body, the ordinary World of Aging is inescapable. Things age in linear time.

When you look into a mirror, you see your body at a specific age, and you see the physical effects of that age. But when you close your physical eyes, you have no age. Your mindset is so powerful that it can create physical representation—in other words, "You are as old as you think." Mind always trumps body.

Agelessness is a new positioning of the locus of consciousness that is completely empowering. People who are aware of just this one reality will look and feel younger. This is more than the awareness that I am not my body—it is the awareness that I am a self that contains the physical body to which I am attached right now. We are back to nothing again. We have returned to the third key.

Our bodies are merely earth suits—not unlike an astronaut's space suit—made up mostly of water. When you are a guest on this planet, you relate to yourself and others as if we are our earth suits. You misidentify who you are. You are energy, space, and light—much more than a lump of meat, bone, and blood.

You have a body—an earth suit. You need an earth suit to exist on earth just like an astronaut needs a space suit to survive in the vacuum of outer space. But you are not your earth suit. If you believe you are, you lose the space of nothing! If you choose, you can be the possibility of an ever new life, no matter the age of your earth suit.

Actions

Emptying is a pathway to creating nothing. Do the following exercise and record your insights in your Phoenix journal.

1. In your environment, what could you get rid of? Look in your garage, your closet, your office, and other areas. Start to clear out the things you don't really need.

2. What do you do that it would serve you to stop doing? Stop doing it right away! Ask a friend if you don't see anything.

3. Who are you being that it doesn't serve you to be? Are you ready to let go of being that way? (Examples might include being angry, being sad, or being guilty.) Let go! Ask a friend if you don't see anything.

4. What recurring thoughts no longer serve you? (For example, "I'm no good.") Are you willing to let these thoughts go? Are you willing to give them up? When are you willing to give them up?

5. Recall times when you weren't there. There was just space. You were in the zone. There was just flow. Sit quietly and recapture that experience. Repeat this exercise daily for a week.

CHAPTER 11

Create Your Ageless Self—Create Your Unique Soul Song

I think it's a mistake to ever look for hope outside of one's self.
I tried to die near the end of the war. The same dream returned
each night until I dared not go to sleep and grew quite ill.
I dreamed I had a child, and even in the dream I saw it was
my life, and it was an idiot, and I ran away. But it always crept onto
my lap again, clutched at my clothes, until I thought, if I could kiss it,
whatever in it was my own, perhaps I could sleep. And I bent
to its broken face, and it was horrible ... but I kissed it.
I think one must finally take one's life in one's arms.

— Arthur Miller

B EFORE YOU BEGIN TO USE THE FOURTH KEY—to create yourself and your unique soul song—let's review your practice of the first three keys.

You began by choosing an ageless life for yourself—a departure from the normal agreement about aging—and you committed to your choice. You chose to be ageless. You realized that who you've normally been in life is a myth—the myth of Me. You are not your body. You are not your past; you are not the sum total of what has happened to you. You are not that reactive self; that Me, personality, or ego is nothing but an invented illusion.

The Phoenix left its old life to bring forth an ageless life. Just like the Phoenix, you have begun to leave your old life by the key of completion. You emptied yourself of regrets, resentments, incompletions, and the limitations of who you thought yourself to be. You created an experience of nothing and began a transformation from aging to ageless.

You let go of the known and are willing to exist in the space of nothing—which is the space of all possibility. As you experienced being nothing, you emerged as an opening for a new life. You are not the self you have known so well in the past. You are not the Me that has given birth to your ordinary thoughts and feelings. Instead, you are an ageless clearing in which the rest of your life is now pure possibility.

That's all been very important work that has set the stage for what comes next: Now is the time to invent who you will be from this point forward—to invent the you of your future.

This is where you draw your line in the sands of time. Until now, you were on one side of the line—but you just stepped over to the other side. Being on the old side was automatic and reactive, and this new side requires you to create yourself on a continuous, ongoing basis. Without this ongoing creation you will slip back into your ordinary way of being—your normal life.

That all sounds exciting. But exactly how do you create yourself?

Let me share what happened when I stepped over the line to create a new Me. When I was in high school—on one side of the line—I was a completely nonathletic nerd. Today—on the other side of the line—my home contains trophies and certificates representing the state, national, and world sporting events I have won and records I have broken.

What precipitated that change? When I went into the U.S. Marines, I had to step over the line and become athletic; I had no choice. I wasn't the only one facing this dilemma: Every day with our basic training squad, we practiced looking at ourselves differently than in the past. I knew if I was ever going to change, I needed to speak about myself differently. There was absolutely no room for repeating my ordinary conversation about what a nerd I was. In fact in the Marine Corps you are given a new conversation about who you are and will be.

In the Marines you follow orders. I did what I was told; it didn't matter if I thought I couldn't do it. Day after brutal day, we learned to think about ourselves—talk to ourselves—in a new way. As my behavior changed, so did the way I talked about myself, to myself and others. That's an important part of the process: You create your new self by speaking who you are to yourself and others.

As I started talking about myself differently, my endurance and strength improved dramatically. And as I saw those improvements, I became very interested in physical fitness and endurance training.

Like the Phoenix, once you have crossed the line of demarcation required by transformation, you can create and manifest a new life. As a human being, you are unique among all other creatures because you create with language—with your word.

You are now face to face with the opportunity to create yourself newly from the ashes of your past, and you will create the new you with your word.

Is it possible that you know nothing about yourself right now? In the past, what have you known to be true about you? What have you known about your own limits? What have you said about who you are? Are you willing to step over the line? You have seen yourself only based on your own interpretations. Are you willing to bring forth a new you from the ashes? Are you willing to see the magnificent future of who you could be? Are you willing to know nothing about yourself and then create yourself newly?

You can do it, and it takes practice.

This is not the same as thinking about the person of your past. You will be creating the you of your future. You create yourself by saying who you are newly until you can own it. Affirmations normally don't go deep enough. Each time you affirm "I am wealthy" on top of "I am always broke," for example, it simply reminds you of how broke you are. Donald Trump doesn't have to affirm "I am wealthy"—it's who he is!

Example is a powerful teacher, so I'd like to share another example of how I once transformed myself with new words. As you read my description, think about some times in your life that may have been similar.

You have to see who you have been being before you have a choice about who you could be. That was important for me. Until I was thirty-five, I avoided public speaking because I believed the words I always used to describe myself: "I'm shy." As a high school principal in Watsonville, California, I had many opportunities to speak to groups, such as the Rotary Club or P.T.A., and I often declined those invitations, inventing stories about my many conflicting engagements.

Whenever I did accept an invitation, I spent days preparing and worrying about a twenty- or thirty-minute talk I was to give. I was so afraid that I'd say something stupid or look silly—but more than that, once I said I was shy, I truly believed it from then on. Shy wasn't just a thought—it described who I was. It was just as descriptive as saying, "My eyes are hazel and I am shy." Painful, awkward, and worried feelings backed up my self-talk.

Then while participating in a self-development program, I had an epiphany! I realized I am not inherently shy. I had just always said I am shy. I don't even remember when I first began to say it, but I finally realized that my repeated saying of it made it so. My unquestioned saying was the jailer—and when I saw that, I took the keys back!

When I realized the limiting nature of "I am shy" and saw that it was part of the myth about me, I also realized the choice was mine: I had the power to create a new way of being. I trained myself to become a public speaker. Sure enough, I found out that a person doesn't become a competent public speaker because of an inherent character trait or a genetic ability. To become a good public speaker you choose to do it—in spite of your previous self-defeating conversation—then you train and you practice.

Compared to the person convinced he was shy, I scarcely recognize myself. I now have spoken publicly to groups of people from all walks of life, of different religions, of different economic backgrounds, of different ages, and with different agendas. I have now spoken to people with different world views and from many different cultures—including Native Americans, Aboriginals, Maoris, Asians, Europeans, Middle-Easterners, gang members, and government officials. Through translators I spoke Chinese, Japanese, German, Spanish, Swedish, French, Russian, Lebanese, Hindi, and Hebrew for days at a time.

Most important, I am free to express my intention and make a difference with my speaking now that my imaginary "I am shy" isn't in my way. By eliminating just that one limit, a whole new world opened up for me.

We all get trapped in beliefs about ourselves, just like I was trapped in the belief that I was shy. In reality, those beliefs are only limiting superstitions. If you don't recognize a superstition, it's a true superstition, and you will go on living as if it is real! You will live an unreal life in an unreal world, thinking it's real. What gets tragically lost is the gift of who you really are—your unique soul song.

Like the Phoenix, you are one of a kind—a wondrous creation of the universe. And you have the power to create yourself with your word. What is specifically different about you? What unique song from your higher self would you like to sing? What variation to that song would you like to explore? It all starts with saying who you will be.

Here are some thoughts from some great thinkers to prime the pump in designing your new self. You shouldn't automatically believe them, but ponder these thoughts along with the other things you've considered so far.

If we all did the things we are capable of doing, we would literally astound ourselves.

— Thomas Edison

Does it really work for us to go through our lives as though there was no realization beyond the grasp of our system of concepts, the experience of which would transform the quality of our lives?

— Werner Erhard

To be sure, a human being is a finite being and his freedom is restricted. The most important aspect is not the freedom from the conditions, but the freedom to take a stand toward the conditions.

— Viktor E. Frankl

I have not the shadow of a doubt that any man or woman could achieve what I have achieved, if he or she would make the same effort and cultivate the same hope and faith.

— Gandhi

You are the Creator. Whatever you believe, that is what you create and that is what you become.

— Gurudev

As human beings, we create the reality of who we are by speaking it into existence. Given the vast importance of this inherent power, it behooves us to examine deeply the unconscious patterns of our own speaking and claim the sacred gift to create ourselves and our world with our words. Creating with our word is the access to our divinity.

— Ron Zeller

Who Do You Choose to Be?

You can create something from nothing. You can create "I am" or you can create "I am not." You can create "Life is great," or you can create "Life stinks." You can create being a player in the game, or you can create watching the game from the comfort of your seat in the stands with the rest of the crowd. You can create playing ordinary games or you can create playing impossible, extraordinary, and adventurous games. *Who do you choose to be?*

Life is the unlimited potential for experience. What experiences will you choose? Making a potent choice is the fundamental requisite of bringing forth power. Will you choose to generate new and fulfilling experiences? Will you choose a life of mastery, or will you settle for your usual reactions to the circumstances life dealt you and you created? Will you stay stuck in past conclusions, beliefs, and feelings, such as "I can't," "I don't know how," "He's to blame, it's not my fault," or "I'm not good enough, smart enough, pretty enough, thin enough, fat enough, lovable enough, young enough—I'm just not enough."

Will you fly or will you hide in the ashes of an ordinary nest? Dare to create yourself being uniquely extraordinary and magnificent. Expand your repertoire! Dare to create yourself transfigured!

In creating you, you are somewhat limited by being a human being—the same way a fish is limited by the fact that fish live in water. Let's expand your view of who you are and who you can invent yourself to be by first looking at your humanity. I suspect you don't know who you really are, and that can leave you in a big mess.

What is a human being? How is a human being distinct from everything else? Most religious scriptures teach us that human beings have a God-like power to create. Consider the biblical scripture, "In the beginning was the Word, and the Word was with God, and the Word was God. The same was in the beginning with God. All things were made by him; and without him was not any thing made that was made." (John 1:1–3). We might also understand that to mean that as humans, we create our world. When human beings are in agreement, they can create a whole world. For example, for many centuries people believed that the earth was the center of the universe; that was not real, of course, but it was a "real" world at the time created by humanity's agreement.

This is an important thing to realize about human beings: They are not like anything else in the world since they have the power to create with their word.

What you say is the beginning of manifesting. With your word, expressed to yourself or others, you bring into existence whole new worlds of meaning. With your word, you bring forth yourself. Who do you say you are?

Though your word is your access to power, your word doesn't necessarily have power. Only a word that is whole, perfect, and complete has power. If your word has no power, you can't reliably create yourself as a person transformed, distinct from your past. Most people don't pay much attention to their word; they give it cheaply and don't give a thought to honoring their word. Most of us don't consistently do what we say we will do, even when our health is at stake. You may have to reclaim the power of your word to create with it.

To repeat, without the power of your word, you can't create. Without the power to create, all that remains is reaction. You stay stuck in the familiar patterns of your life using your word to describe and explain why you can't have

Creating a new and unpredictable reality. Winning the U.S. National Championship and on the way to a World Championship four years later.

what you want. In other words, you're just like an animal, except you're able to explain your failures and frustrations. Without the power of your word, you go down the river of life without oars; you are merely adrift and reacting to currents. The difference between you and a rock is that when you both roll down a hill, the rock just rolls. You explain why you are rolling all the way down.

Empowering Yourself with Your Word: Integrity

To create yourself newly, your word must have power. Unfortunately, most of us have lost the power of our word. Consider the New Year's resolution phenomenon as proof: We make a "resolution," saying we are going to accomplish what we haven't been able to accomplish before. Those who do manage to change usually do so for only a short period of time—then it's back to business as usual.

With the power of your word you first declare who you will be, then sustain your creation, and finally take action to manifest it. Without the power of your word, you are doomed to continually reacting in your same ordinary limited ways, merely imagining and pretending that you have a choice about who you will be or what you will accomplish.

The dictionary defines integrity as being whole, perfect, and complete. If you have integrity, then, your word is whole, perfect, and complete. Being one who can create requires that your word have power—and that you have integrity.

Restoring Your Integrity

Integrity is not to be confused with morality, although the lack of integrity often accompanies a lack of morality and vice versa. Morality is about values, judgments, and personal added meaning. Integrity is about honoring your word and having your word be whole, perfect, and complete.

You're not good if you have integrity. You're not bad if you don't have integrity. Good and bad are cultural judgments and descriptions. When your integrity gives you the power to create, others will probably judge that you are a good person. Yet integrity has nothing to do with the judgments of good or bad, right or wrong.

Human beings can probably never maintain absolute integrity. But you can keep your promises and commitments on a daily basis and clean up your word when broken—and in the process, you can access a life of integrity. Having a commitment to integrity and honoring your word is the source of having the power of your word and thus being able to create and manifest a whole new level of extraordinary results. Having integrity gives you the power to act in order to have what you say you want. It allows you to generate results beyond your imagination.

Examine your life. Look for areas and situations in which you are not honoring your word. Make an actual list. Clean up your integrity wherever it has been compromised. Communicate to those with whom you have not kept your word, ask for forgiveness and make new promises. Put those promises into a physical structure; in other words, make a list—what you will do, by when it will be complete, and with whom you are making the agreement. Write it down! It is not real if it doesn't exist in the physical world. Your mind will want to avoid this project like the plague. Do it anyway. Integrity is the access to the full magnitude of who you are. It's worth the discomfort and the confrontation in dealing with any instance where integrity is missing.

Example Integrity List

Let's look at an example of a simple integrity list. Here are some of the things many of us do or don't do that violate our integrity:

1. Not getting regular dental checkups.
2. Ignoring car repairs.
3. Eating too much junk food.
4. Breaking exercise agreements.
5. Stealing supplies or tools from work.
6. Allowing people to borrow books without returning them.
7. Not paying or cheating on taxes.
8. Ignoring parking tickets.
9. Not paying back money borrowed—and not communicating about it.
10. Disregarding important emails.
11. Failing to update a voicemail message.
12. Storing more and more junk in the garage.
13. Not returning telephone calls as promised.

14. Not completing and restoring your word when you have broken it.
15. Abusing drugs.
16. Cheating on a partner.
17. Not telling the truth when it's inconvenient.
18. Not keeping your promises to your children and pretending they won't notice.
19. Breaking your word with yourself.
20. Not doing things the way you know they are meant to be done.

We all have areas in which we haven't kept our word with ourselves or others. We all have times where we have tolerated a lack of integrity. What if we each operated with total integrity? The entire world would dramatically shift!

Engaging in this integrity awareness and cleanup campaign leaves you with joy, satisfaction, peace, space, and the power to create the life you have always wanted, no matter what your age. When you live inside the World of Ageless Living, cleaning up your integrity is an ongoing process. The power of your word is restored. You recover your godlike powers to create.

In life, you have a choice: You can continue as the same old 'Me' or, with the power of your word, you can successfully create a new you. I find it interesting that people seem to resist their own magnificence more than anything—yet if you ever discover who you really are, it will move you to tears. You are magnificent, immortal, and unique—one of a kind. And the way to realize that is to clean up your life.

Consider what it would be like to live in a world that is whole, perfect, and complete—a life in which you, your relationships, and the power of your word are whole, perfect, and complete. When you tolerate missing integrity, you will experience struggle and effort. Where integrity exists, you will experience being able to create and have a life of treasured values such as love, peace, kindness, passion, joy and self-discipline.

This whole chapter is about using the power of your word to bring forth a *you* other than the you you've been up until now. You are bringing forth an ageless you by naming that as a possibility. Let's complete this chapter with some actions and practicies to make real your ability to apply and use this information.

Actions

The actions below allow you to restore the power of your word—and the power of your word allows you to create yourself newly. Without creating a new *you*, you continue to be a reaction machine—stuck in the past, a *thing* that is aging.

1. Make an integrity list. This can include broken promises that you have made to yourself and others as well as promises others have made to you that have not been kept or completed.

2. For each item in your list, make a note on what it will take to clean it up and restore integrity.

3. Go to work on completing the items on your list; watch your ageless life expand as you do.

4. Review your unique soul song, a contribution or a difference you are drawn to make in life.

To live in the World of Ageless Living, make cleaning up your life an ongoing practice.

CHAPTER 12

Cause and Manifest Your Phoenix Future

However bad life may seem, there is always something you can do,
and succeed at. While there's life, there is hope.

— Stephen Hawking

Y OU ARE NOW like the rising Phoenix and ready to take flight. You've let go of your history as that which defined you, you've become a space from which you can intentionally invent yourself newly and cause the rest of your life to be the best of your life. You are ready to use the fifth key of the Phoenix Myth which allows you to cause and manifest a new future of extraordinary quality.

Creating a Phoenix future, an amazing life with great results, requires the courage to give up the habit of automatic thoughtless reaction. It also demands you take on the risk and responsibility of conscious creation.

What you're about to do will break all the "rules" you're used to living. Consider this: Your life has a certain predictable trajectory—a probable future. None of us can say precisely what's going to happen in the future, but unless you make some dramatic changes, your future is likely to be very similar to your past. There might be some subtle differences, but it's probably going to be more of the same. If you don't believe that, look at what life insurance companies do: They can't say with absolute certainty how long you're going to live—but they can generate a life insurance policy based on your likely life span, predicting how long you'll live using all kinds of factors based on your past and a current physical exam.

The Phoenix future you're about to create is a new possibility of you, not an extension of your past.

Creating a new future is not an easy thing to do. Have you ever tried to tone your body into one you love, learn to play a musical instrument, or master a new language? Then you understand that old habits are powerful; in fact, they can seem insurmountable. The very wiring of your brain fights against the kind of breakthrough you need to make. It's the same kind of struggle that occurs when you try to drive on the opposite side of the road in a different country—the first time you try, your brain seems to tilt! The short-term memory is wired to struggle with change and innovation. The patterns of your past will be relentless in demanding that you return to doing things the same way you always have—a type of survival instinct. Only when you establish new pathways in your long-term memory will new ways of thinking and doing things become effortless and comfortable. You'll become unconsciously competent.

If you think that sounds difficult, you're right. It takes committed, consistent practice to rewire the neuron patterns in your brain. Legendary Indiana University head basketball coach Bobby Knight was well acquainted with the struggle as he tried to elevate his team's performance. In his frustration, he quipped, "Everyone wants to be a champion, but nobody wants to practice."

It's *practice* that builds the champion—regardless of the specific endeavor—and practice at first is not comfortable. All great accomplishment depends on being driven by passion to make a difference instead of simply giving in to comfort.

You need to understand that we're not used to being driven by passion. That's just not the way we're built. Our brain is designed to keep things the same and keep life predictable. Our brain is a prediction machine. We are automatically run by the same beliefs, thoughts, and emotions over and over. That describes your past: You have survived life's dangers, real or imagined, by being what you now know as *Me*. Those patterns of being, now associated with your survival, are automatic.

Here's how it works: You look in the mirror one day and say, "I'm going to exercise and lose these extra twenty pounds." Almost immediately you have the thought, "I'm too busy today; I'll start exercising tomorrow." "Tomorrow" becomes the day after tomorrow, and then the next week, and then the next month. In fact, the exercise never happens. What does happen is an automatic thought that always provides another believable reason why you can't take new action now. And if by some miracle the exercise does happen, it is seldom sustained. Our neurological wiring drives us back to business as usual.

Until now, your life has been controlled by this system, even though you were almost certainly unaware of it. You may not realize what is happening, but you listen to your thoughts and believe them as if they reliably tell you what's real. That's not all: You also have feelings aligned with your thoughts, and accept both as if they are you. Your life then becomes about the automatic continuance of your habits and patterns. It's a powerful autonomic system that keeps you the same so the familiar you survives. You then live in the box of life rather than in the adventure of life.

What we've just described explains exactly why information alone seldom has the power to change your future. If you're addicted to tobacco, you won't even be fazed by a warning label on a package of cigarettes—even if it says you might die from smoking. Millions of smokers keep smoking despite the potential damage to their health—and all the warning labels. And those millions of people have very good "reasons" to justify the habit.

How many good "reasons" do you have to justify your habits? Most of us have them. They signify what I call a "reasonable life"—a sad situation in which reasons determine the quality of life. In his book *Maxims for Revolutionists*, Nobel prize-winner George Bernard Shaw wrote, "The reasonable man adapts himself to the world; the unreasonable one persists in trying to adapt the world to himself. Therefore all progress depends on the unreasonable man."

In exercising the fifth key, your word must have power; authenticity is a critical element. You have the power of creation when what you say is who you are. Your word and your actions become inextricably aligned when you relate to your word as if it matters that's what I mean by authenticity.

Make no mistake: It's difficult to bring yourself forth newly. But make no mistake about this either: It is possible. Regardless of how difficult it is, you can escape from the box—the paradigm of aging.

Causing Your "Created" Future

Creating a new future begins with inventing a clear vision of that future. More than a simple prediction, it involves being who you will be in that new future. Does that new future call you to be—generous, creative, ageless, adventurous, alive, healthy, energetic, passionate, charismatic, joyful, and productive? New actions are necessary for this unpredictable future and these new results. As you learned in the fourth key, you have to be willing to give up thinking you really know who you are—for instance, "I'm a failure"—to create yourself newly. To create new results in your life outside of what's normal is an existential act of courage.

If anything is possible, what new life would you give yourself? Consider all the domains that are important to human beings—intimate relationships, finances, career, or spiritual, physical, mental, emotional, or social well-being, to name a few. Focus on who you will be, not what you will do or have. What does your life look like if the best is still ahead of you?

Talk about yourself as if you are living in this possible future now. Here are just a few examples: I am a powerful global leader. I am wealthy. I am fit and well. I am a doctor. I am calm and peaceful. I am an author. I am spiritual. I am loving.

Exercise in Visualizing Your Ageless Phoenix Future

Complete the following sentences:

My created Phoenix future (extraordinary, unpredictable life) looks like this three years from now...

Review what you have written. Is it still an extension of your past? If so, rewrite it, inventing an even more out there Phoenix future. It takes practice to get out of the box of our own minds.

Continuing further, my greatest life five years from now includes...

Considering what I have created so far and looking further at a magnificent future, I see...

Taking this even further, one possible perfect life for me is...

A possible life in which I am making a difference or contributing to humanity one year from now includes...

Breaking Free—Impossible Games™

Why on earth do some of us choose to attempt something we can't possibly do? Because when you invent something impossible to accomplish—something that would light you up and inspire you if you succeeded, you can become a player in a brand new game—an Impossible Game™. Winning your new game destroys who your mind thinks you are, leaving you with a power to operate beyond your normal limits. It's one of the best ways to get outside the boundaries of Me. But you have to play your game of impossibility as if your life depends on it, because to create a new life it does.

I did exactly that in my own life when I chose to play a game I could never win—an Impossible Game™. Here's what happened.

After I became free of pain and apparently had reversed the progress of the cancer in my stomach in 1995, I could honestly call myself a cancer survivor. But I was still gripped by the fear of cancer. I believed I had gotten cancer because I had worked too hard. It made sense, then, to take it easy. My life became about taking it easy.

I was taking it easy to avoid dying—but in taking it so easy, I had died to life. I was avoiding the risk that comes with being fully engaged in living. I had to somehow trick my mind into accepting that I was undeniably well. I decided to do something so bizarre that if I succeeded, my brain would have to conclude that I was cured—not just a cancer survivor. So I registered for the Wasatch Front 100 Mile Endurance Run held in Utah. This race is for ultra-fit athletes. I believe I was the least ultra-fit of anyone who has ever run this race for the last twenty five years.

The Wasatch 100 is a race through the mountains of Utah, run at an average elevation of 8,500 feet, with 50,000 feet of elevation changes as participants run up and down the mountains of the Wasatch Range. The race begins about fifty miles north of Salt Lake City and ends in or near Sundance, Utah. You can imagine what the experience is like from its nickname: "100 Miles of Heaven and Hell." This race is still run each year. Here's how it's described on the Internet:

> The Wasatch Front 100 is one of the most uniquely challenging ultra-running events in the world. It is a study in contrasts—peaks and valleys, trail and scree, heat and cold, wet and dry, summer and winter, day and night, Desolation Lake and Point Supreme, "I can't" and "I will!" Dickens had the Wasatch in mind when he wrote, "It was the best of times; it was the worst of times." The primitive and isolated nature of the course is both its beauty and its challenge. It requires the individual runner to rely primarily on himself or herself rather than the race's support systems. The Wasatch 100 is not just a race of distance and speed; it is an immersion in adversity, adaptation and perseverance.

My first day of training in Tarrytown, New York, was just outside a Holiday Inn. I ran a block and I was utterly winded. I found myself laughing hysterically, thinking I had to be a total nut case for signing up for this race at age sixty-five while recovering from cancer and having the fitness level of a three-year-old. Nevertheless, I trained for six months, averaging two hours a day, until the day of the race arrived. At that point I could jog, walk, and run fifteen miles on mountain trails. I was actually proud of myself; I reasoned that running just twenty miles of the race would be a real victory. My plan was to drop out after twenty miles. I never imagined I could run one hundred miles in the time allowed.

The race began September 7 at 5:00 in the morning. In addition to the expected challenges of the race, I had a bad cold. We ran the first three miles of the race up the face of the mountain, ascending from an elevation of 5,000 feet to 9,000 feet. Then we ran twelve more miles to reach the first checkpoint, a big radar dome high above the Salt Lake Valley.

Eighteen miles into the race, I felt pretty good. At mile twenty, I still felt strong and chose to keep going. At mile thirty-five, Mary Louise was at the checkpoint to meet me. She removed my shoes and socks, washed my feet, and massaged PrimaDerma, a Russian adaptogenic herbal ointment, into my feet, calves, and thighs. She gave me a change of shoes and socks and spooned super foods into my mouth. I rehydrated and let race officials weigh me to determine if it was safe for me to continue without risking my life. I passed the test. At this point many runners were dropping out of the competition because of blisters the size of silver dollars on their feet. Their duct-taped feet were raw and bleeding.

Those of us left in the race pushed on to the next checkpoint at mile fifty. I couldn't believe that by early evening I had covered fifty miles on mountain trails. I was exhausted but decided to keep going.

The next twenty-five miles were slow and agonizing. Arriving at the Brighton Ski Resort checkpoint, I was beyond totally burned out. It was 4 a.m. and I was shuffling along at one mile an hour. My pacer and friend, Julio Garreaud—whose job it was to keep me going—said with real concern, "Maybe you should drop out." I decided he was right. I planned to quit after they weighed me at the ski resort checkpoint and then sleep for a week.

After the weigh-in, I sat down; with my eyes closed, I ate the food Mary Louise was pushing into my mouth. I was wiped out—finished. I didn't have an ounce of energy left. As soon as my stomach was full, I passed out. Mary Louise worked on my feet again as I slept.

I woke up, not knowing where I was or how long I had been asleep. I was aware only of two feet in the middle of my back pushing me upright. It was Mary Louise. "Look, you old fart," she told me, "you said you were going to do one hundred miles. You've only done seventy-five. Get your butt back out on the trail and get going." Mary Louise can be quite the bulldog at times.

The next thing I knew I was on the trail climbing up to 11,000 feet, one miserable step after another. It was the hardest thing I have ever done! Only the dogged perseverance of my pacer Paul Schmidt kept me moving.

I reached the summit of my climb as the sun came up. Then a strange thing happened—I got more energy! A few minutes later, I felt a little more energy! Somehow, some way, my empty tank was getting refilled. I ended up jogging and running the rest of the way to the finish line. I successfully completed the race and opened up a door to a new world and a new Me. I had become an ultramarathoner.

Next, I traveled to the Annapurna range in the Himalayan Mountains, where I ran and trekked halfway around this three-hundred-mile mountain range at very high elevations.

My next challenge was the Inca Trail in Peru, originating near Cusco and ending in the famed archeological site of Machu Picchu. I ran and jogged through forests and up endless high stone steps to the sacred city. This trek was one of the most grueling ordeals yet one of the most magnificent adventures I have ever experienced. Mary Louise and I camped out in nightly deluges and cold temperatures and awoke to the glory of some of the most amazing views we have ever seen. Coming through the Sun Gate and seeing Machu Picchu for the first time was one of the most stunning moments of my life.

The Grand Canyon was another memorable run. I ran down one side of the canyon, across the floor, and up the other side. The unique, colorful, and vast panoramic views moved me profoundly. At some point, my awareness shifted from being a thing running to being a space of running. I lost my sense of self and became the awareness of magnificent splendor. The borders between me as the observer and the world that I observed disappeared.

Are you ready to play an Impossible Game™? Here are the fundamentals:

1. Choose a game that, if you win, will blow your mind.

2. Be clear about the outcome—what constitutes winning but looks impossible.

3. Create a sticky conversation about your game with yourself and others—a conversation that keeps you in sustainable action.

4. Choose a coach that you say will have you succeed at your Impossible Game™.

5. Assemble a team that will empower you to win your game. They need to be engaged with you not well wishers.

6. Play your game with everything you've got.

7. Keep reexamining how to most effectively forward your game as you are playing. Be willing to give up everything you know about how to win this game.

Naming—Another Access to Causing Your Newly Adventurous, Joyful, and Exciting Phoenix Future

According to the Torah, God told Adam to dress and maintain the physical space known as the Garden of Eden. God also commanded Adam to "name the animals." This was an extraordinarily unique event, because the name you give something dictates your reaction to it thereafter. When Adam named the horse "a leaping thing," he created a different future relationship with that animal than if he had named it "a delectable lunch."

If I name a man "my enemy," I respond to him differently than if I name him "my friend." By naming, we literally create a linguistic event that adds meaning which shapes and dictates our future perceptions. From that point forward, we perceive only what we expect. There is no longer space for creation—only repeated predictable reactions.

Adolf Hitler used the power of naming when he said, "The Jews are the cause of all the economic problems in Germany." He created a world of vicious meaning and made his meaning real to many others in his world. In that world, they could justify the atrocities of the Holocaust to themselves. Their actions made perfect sense to them inside the frame of reference created by that naming.

Naming is a powerful creative act that either opens up or absolutely limits all possibility. In fact, the power to name may be the most compelling power we have as human beings. When people name others things like "revolutionaries," "the enemy," "socialists," "fanatics," "insurgents," "terrorists," or "infidels," those so named can be marginalized—things to be separate from, leaving the namer in a disconnected world.

Like the rest of humankind since his time, Adam didn't realize that by naming things he wasn't merely describing them, but was creating them. When Adam ate from the tree of good and evil, he began to name things, "good" or "bad." He even named himself "bad" when he discovered his own nakedness.

Since the creation of the world view of good and bad, we have been polarized and stuck in a massive descriptive naming of everything, including ourselves! As a result, only certain ways of being are available to us. The truth is that there are many ways you can be—and as you come forth from the ashes, you can create yourself in a whole new way. Naming yourself newly will cause you to relate to yourself newly.

Applying the Power of Naming

To capture the power of naming to cause and manifest your extraordinary Phoenix future, examine how you presently apply naming in your life. At some point you named yourself "Me." You then disappeared, and you became a fixed thing. You also named you "I," and the real you disappeared. You became inaccurately known to yourself; you became a thing described by different names. For example: "I am an American," "I am Christian," "Republican," "Conservative," "Mason," "Harvard alumni," "Yuppie," etc. Because of what you named yourself, others relate to you as a fixed thing. (Think of all the people in your life who would get really upset if you dramatically changed who they normally believe you are. They all expect you to continue to stay the same!)

Complete the following sentence:

Who I am is ...

Consider the automatic conversations you use from having named yourself, others, or different aspects of life. Don't think about what you should say; instead, see what you have said and repeatedly say.

To discover some of your unconscious naming, complete the following:

My mother is always ...

My father never ...

Terrorists are ...

My spouse or significant other is ...

I am ...

Women (or men) are ...

What annoys me the most about women (or men) is ...

The government is ...

The one thing about people I don't like is ...

The meaning of life is ...

In the future I will be ...

Your brain repeats these thoughts as if they are true—as if it is describing reality—when it is actually repeatedly dictating to you a self-created version of reality. Who did all the naming that created those thoughts? You did—and your past naming has created and maintained your version of reality.

Here's the worst of it. Your version of reality determines who you can be, what you can do, and what you can have. Are you willing to give up all your past naming of yourself for a new you? Many people find that a scary proposition, to not know themselves—what would I be then?

Use Naming to Give Yourself a New Ageless Future

Complete and write down the following sentences using naming that will provide you with an amazing future. This is more than describing your future—it is committing to who you will be in the future. You are literally inventing your future with naming.

I stand for . . .

My life is about . . .

My greatest accomplishment will be . . .

In life, I'm letting go of being . . .

My three main comittments in life are . . .

The opportunity of my life is . . .

To manifest this new future of extraordinary accomplishment will require new actions. It's time to find out how to design your new future.

Key Five—Causing and Manifesting Results Beyond the Predictable

In the Phoenix Myth, the newly emergent youthful Phoenix created extraordinary results, transforming itself from being old and alone to creating a new beginning of youthfulness. It then led all the other birds on a pilgrimage from Heliopolis to the sun god's altar. The various versions of the myth have had profound impact on many different cultures. More than two thousand years after the myth was created, Heliopolis still exists.

What's next for you now is to cause extraordinary ageless results. The World of Aging is mostly about declining results. The World of Ageless Living is about ever-expanding results.

You can play any game—including an Impossible Game™—that you imagine you can win. Choose to do it, commit to succeed at it, and consistently take appropriate action toward winning. Start with a conversation that describes your game clearly—you can add stickness to your conversation by the following:

- Share your game
- Get a coach
- Find a partner
- Get into action
- Imagine and visualize winning

A Final Thought on Causing and Manifesting Results

Using the power of naming, you can create and name a new world—the World of Ageless Living—where you cause astounding results. When you dare to declare ageless a possibility, you are inventing a new life with that declaration. The rest of your life will be the best of your life. Your powerful speaking can also transform what you used to believe about yourself and free you from the World of Aging. Once you are free, you can take powerful action to manifest extraordinary results.

Actions

1. Write down examples of naming from your life and discern what you now understand about the

dark side of naming (for example, where naming has trapped you and others). Examples: I am broken, I am a looser, life sucks, I'm no good with money.

2. Speak the declarations below, saying them out loud to yourself in the mirror. Speak to yourself in the mirror until you recognize your power to create with your word—to have something exist because you say so.

> Who I am is ageless.
>
> The best is yet to come.
>
> I am not a personality or an identity; I have a personality or an identity.
>
> My energy is unlimited.
>
> The longer I live, the more I contribute.
>
> I shall rise up like a Phoenix from these circumstances.

3. Examine the future you will have caused by creating an Impossible Game™ and describe it. List what critical actions will manifest the you required to win this game.

4. Review and update your integrity list from chapter 11. Look to see what else you need to do to restore your integrity (the power of your word).

CHAPTER 13

Connection—The Key to Sanity

When a mother sits by her infant's cradle,
he [the Phoenix] stands on the pillow,
and, with his wings,
forms a glory around the infant's head.
— Hans Christian Anderson

A S WE EXAMINE the Phoenix Myth, we learn about an immortal bird and how it interrupted the drift of aging. But again consider this: the Phoenix is simply an archetype for human beings, and the code hidden in the myth reveals how we can gloriously sail the sea of aging instead of being ready to sink with a broken mast.

The Phoenix may be a mythical creature, but it represents you and me—and we have much to learn from this legend that in fact applies to our real lives.

One of the strongest messages in the myth is that of connectedness. Look at the excerpt above from Hans Christian Anderson's "The Phoenix"—the Phoenix is illuminating and acknowledging the connection between a mother and her baby. Generally in our world, a mother and her baby are about as naturally connected as it's possible to be. You may be personally acquainted with a woman who was planning to place her child for adoption but changed her mind because it was simply too painful to sever that connection.

Does that kind of powerful connectedness apply only to a mother and her baby? Or does it describe our natural feelings toward each other? I suggest we are all connected; it's our natural state. That may not seem to be the case when you consider that even those in intimate or familial relationships attempt to control and dominate each other. And there's the fact that at any given time, the nations of this world are engaged in an average of forty wars. Given evidence like that, how can we even imagine that we are all connected?

Here's why I believe we are all connected and why that's a natural state: When you eliminate anything that separates you from someone who is close to you, what's left? Love. Pure, simple love. In fact, we use the word **love** to express the experience of connectedness.

You don't have to try to get connected; you just have to get rid of what's between you and another to realize it. As self-development master Werner Erhard said, "You don't have to go looking for love when it's where you come from." To live disconnected and alone is to be old, whatever your age—and to end up alone, separate, and disconnected is insanity. A participant in the World of Ageless Living eliminates disconnectedness, expands the experience of love, and becomes more aware of their connectedness with others.

We live in a high-tech age of apparent connection. The key to real connection is found in values such as kindness, compasion, forgiveness, understanding, and especially communication. Unfortunately, most communication by virtue of its design maintains disconnectedness and promotes the delusion of being a separate thing.

I once led a communication and self-development workshop in San Jose, California that was attended by some of the most brilliant people from around the world. These people worked at some of the leading technology companies—corporations like Adobe, Apple, Cisco, Google, Intel, and Xerox, to name just a few. They invested their intellect and energy in developing tools for the worldwide revolution in electronic communication. Yet these brilliant pioneers in communication who spoke incessantly through text messages, email, Twitter, Facebook, and blogs were actually some of the loneliest, most isolated, disconnected people on the planet. All of the electronic "communication" that seemed to connect people was a profound failure when it came to giving them the experience of being related.

As the workshop unfolded, these isolated people were willing to talk to people authentically face to face sharing their feelings and experiences. When they did, they rediscovered the love, joy, and deep appreciation of others that comes from realizing their connectedness.

As you look at the sixth key, you declare, "Giving up what I already know is possible, and giving up who I have unconsciously determined that I am, I stand in the space of nothing and choose to fly with new freedom into a future of ever-expanding love, relationship, and connectedness."

As we examine the Phoenix Myth, we see that the Phoenix is connected to other creatures around the planet—and, in fact, it is connected to life outside of itself. Again, an essential aspect of the Phoenix Code is to assume that all of us as humans are represented by the Phoenix. And since the Phoenix Myth shows us how to deal with aging, each of us, like the Phoenix, must keep expanding our connectedness to realize who we really are. Let us revisit Einstein's quote about who we really are because it so nails the mental state that traps us:

> A human being is part of a whole, called by us, the Universe, a part limited in time and space. He experiences himself, his thoughts and feelings, as something separated from the rest—a kind of optical delusion of his consciousness. This delusion is a kind of prison for us, restricting us to our personal desires and to affection for a few persons nearest us. Our task must be to free ourselves from this prison by widening our circle of compassion to embrace all living creatures and the whole of nature in its beauty.

Notice that Einstein teaches that our separateness, our being disconnected, is only a compelling delusion. But we live as if disconnectedness is reality. To be ageless is to love, relate, and be connected. Our job is to recover our sanity by realizing and expanding the love and compassion already inside us.

Once when I was visiting Montreal, I walked past a transient hotel that was about six stories high. It was a warm day, and from virtually every open window leaned a person slowly drinking a can of beer and smoking a cigarette. It was like going to a TV store and seeing the same show on fifty different TVs.

It occurred to me then how easy it is to end up in our own separate space, watching the game of life instead of playing it. Are you connected with others—***really connected*** and in touch with your experience of love? Or are you watching the world go by from your separate window? As the years go by, is your connectedness expanding or disappearing?

Let's examine your connectedness in your community. The words communication and community come from the same root as communion—a joining together of minds or spirits. Complete the following three sentences:

1. My closest friends in my community are …

2. In my community, I really appreciate …

3. In my community, we are really aligned on …

Now let's take a look at love and affinity in your family. Complete these three sentences:

1. My father always …
2. My mother never …
3. On a scale from one to ten (where ten is bliss and joy), my love for my family is a …

Transforming the Myth of Aging held in Sundance, Utah. Here participants also discovered their connectedness while experiencing community.

Quantum Communication and the Power of Context

How do you access your connection with others? Communication! But I don't mean what normally passes for communication. I'm talking about a new kind of communication—***quantum communication***, the kind that occurs when there is no distance between the people who are communicating. There's no agenda, no fear, no worry, no righteousness, and no judgment—only communication free of personal psychology. People are being together with nothing added.

Quantum communication involves the minimum personal point of view and the maximum space for creating results. It opens the door to a magical life of performance and quality. Quantum communication is causal—one or both people in the conversation are committed to causing. It arises from connectedness, authentic self-expression, aliveness, and the presence of love and empowerment. The power to manifest an extraordinary future is expressed through quantum communication. You don't merely have two things talking to each other; instead, you have a co-created clearing for unexpected and surprising possibilities.

Quantum communication through speaking and listening is the communication of space and possibility. Most of what passes for communication I call Newtonian communication—the communication of things involved in stimulus response. In Newtonian communication, people try to get other people to do what they want them to do or stop people from doing what they don't want them to do. This ordinary kind of communication comes from the view that humans are just merely things in a universe of things. The very structure of Newtonian communication pulls for and maintains our delusion of separateness and disconnection. Quantum physics, on the other hand, has inspired a new model of communication—a model that reflects love, connectedness, and relatedness.

To see what I mean, compare the two:

Newtonian Communication	Quantum Communication
• describes	• creates
• predetermined	• arises in freedom and space
• manipulation, domination, justification	• love, caring, and generosity
• waiting to speak/not listening	• listening
• force	• power
• about survival	• about workability
• being right, making others wrong	• being aligned
• keeps things the same	• new possibility
• being a thing aging	• generates ageless and youthful
• tries to win and avoid losing	• win/win

It is useful to understand the relationship between the context of communication and the content. If your world view is that "life stinks," the content of your communication will be shaped by that world view. It will always be lurking in the background.

It's important to be aware of what contexts are in the background, hidden from our awareness. There are unlimited kinds of contexts and countless points of view from which people communicate. Hollywood has given us some great examples. *Life Stinks* by Mel Brooks illustrates one fundamental view of life; another movie, *Life Is Beautiful*, illustrates the polar opposite, the power of a positive context. It might be useful to watch both movies and contrast their message.

A variation of "life stinks" is the context of "I stink." Inside that mindset, you believe there is something wrong with you. As a result, the content of your communication will reflect that invisible context, and your conversations will mostly be about what is wrong with you and how you are going to fix yourself. Another example of a context is "You stink!" Believing you are fine and everyone else inferior, you feel justified in being separate and ignoring your connectedness.

You can very often see powerful examples of contexts in the workplace. What do you think people mostly talk about at work? Research shows that on the average, 50 percent of the conversations that occur in the American workplace involve gossiping and complaining. That's a normal outcome from the context "life stinks" and "they (managers, owners, other departments) are wrong, stupid, and less than us."

Discovering Your Communication Patterns

Communication is not something you do alone—and it profoundly shapes and impacts our relationships. Answer the questions below in your Phoenix journal, and look for patterns in your communication.

Recall the last time you had an extraordinary conversation.

When was it?

What was it about?

Who was it with?

What made this conversation extraordinary?

What percent of the time would you estimate that you leave a conversation fully satisfied, with nothing incomplete?

Who are you being and what are you concerned with when you are not being powerful or effective in communication?

The previous questions begin to reveal your conversational patterns. Most people are embedded in their conversational habits, blind to the fundamental nature of their communication. People seldom have the opportunity to observe their own communication, so they remain trapped within its unconscious bounds. By observing your normal communication patterns, you have the opportunity to break free of them. You have the opportunity to substitute the elements of quantum communication.

Quantum communication begins with a focused awareness about your Newtonian communication. You begin by asking yourself the question, "What am I up to now as I communicate? What is my underlying agenda?" One predominant and prevalent underlying agenda in communication is to look good and avoid looking bad. Another common behind-the-scenes agenda is to get what we want—or to avoid something we don't want. Still another common agenda is to fix something.

What if your only "agenda" was love? Love is an experience of connectedness. People who live an ageless life have widened their circle of compassion to include those closest to them as well as others. An example of profound and deep love is the perfect love of a mother for her newborn baby; there is a deep, instant bond. I have never been a mother, but I was at the birth of my last son Adam, and I was the first person to hold him and talk to him. As his father, I felt a powerful connection, encompassing deep love, reverence, and an unconditional appreciation of him.

That's not what most people are thinking about when they think of "love." Usually they are talking about a kind of crazy love. "There I was, just walking down the street, and I fell in love. Then a couple of years after we got married, I fell out of love." It's like being a victim—you fall in, you fall out. Just think about the stories you hear in country music: "She stole my heart and stomped it flat!" It sounds like an Incan sacrificial ritual. The lyrics in such songs are crazy but when you hear them enough times, they start to masquerade as truth.

It's amazing to work through your disconnectedness and separateness until you arrive at alignment and community.

It's a very unusual space, but well worth the work. Love is either a concept or an experience. As a concept, it's just a word. As an experience, it's what life is all about.

Exercise: Quantum Communication

In chapter 12, we talked about the power of your word. We spoke about declaring a future with your speaking (declarative speaking) and thereby responsibly creating and manifesting future results. We used naming as a powerful technology for bringing forth a new world, first in language and then in reality.

You already know about quantum communication. You're undoubtedly aware that certain effective leaders—including people like Martin Luther King, Nelson Mandela, Ghandi, Rosa Parks, and John F. Kennedy—created conversations about futures that attracted many people. As a result, many others added their agreement to those conversations, and the visions of these leaders became reality.

These leaders used quantum communication, causing unpredictable things to happen with their speaking. Quantum communication is about communication from *the void*, or the space of nothing. The space of nothing is the space that allows for real creation. From that space, clear intentional meaning can be generated to bring forth a new reality. Just as our greatest leaders create new realities with their word, you also have the power to create new realities with your word.

Complete the following sentences to begin to see how quantum communication can work for you:

My communication is the most effective when ...

When I communicate in a way that grabs people's attention, what's present is ...

What I'm really passionate about in life is ...

My unique song is ...

Now, consider these examples of declarative speaking:

- I'm the one who is going to cause it.
- Trust me to get it done.
- Never mind how much it costs; we'll figure out a way to get the money.
- Thanks for your advice, doctor; I'll take it from here and cause my own recovery.
- I will master Spanish this year.
- This year will be the best year of my life.

Using declarative speaking, write down in your Phoenix journal what your life will now be about. Select something so compelling that your age doesn't matter.

If you were a master communicator, what difference would you choose to have your life make?

Great accomplishment arises from extraordinary communication. Living an ageless life, what are some powerful communications you could share with others?

Actions

Do the following exercises and record your insights in your Phoenix journal. Consider where in your life you will apply these insights.

1. Over the next week, have conversations from being connected that you know you would not ordinarily have.

2. Listen, intending to really understand what the other person is saying and where they are coming from in saying it. If you succeed, you will experience connectedness and love.

3. Share boldly and passionately with three people what your life is really about (your unique song).

4. Practice quantum communication until you can authentically say, "This is a conversation I normally would not have had. The results of this conversation are unprecedented."

CHAPTER 14

Contribution—Singing Your Unique Soul Song

Never forget that you are one of a kind.
Never forget that if there weren't any need for you
in all your uniqueness to be on this earth,
you wouldn't be here in the first place.
...one person can make a difference in the world.
In fact, it is always because of one person that
all the changes that matter in the world
come about. So be that one person.

— Richard Buckminster Fuller

WHILE THE SPECIFICS depend on the culture or country where the Phoenix Myth has been found, the myth contains a subtle message of contribution or service by the Phoenix. Being of service is characteristic of the Phoenix. In some versions of the myth, the feathers of the Phoenix give off light and healing. In other accounts, the Phoenix blesses humanity during their various forms of spiritual practice. In others, it guides birds back to their spirtual home, an altar to the sun in Heliopolis. The

Phoenix also serves the sun god by singing hymns of praise and worship with its beautiful, one-of-a-kind voice. Stories even say that its extraordinary songs caused the sun god Ra to stop his sun chariot in the heavens to listen.

I/we shall rise again better than before is the primary message of the Phoenix Myth for humankind. It is a message of reinvention, renewal, recovery, regeneration, and resurrection—a new rising from total destruction. Inherent in that is the responsibility to serve each other and life; through that service, we encourage each other to reach greater heights together.

The Phoenix Myth reminds us dramatically and sometimes painfully of who we really are. Our spirit—our real self—is summoned from the land of myth when we need it the most. At times like the Phoenix, we especially need to recall our godliness, our powers, our abilities, and our heart. And as the Phoenix reminds us of our glory, it also reminds us that we have opportunities to contribute to each other in life! What amazing self empowerment arises when you choose to contribute, to matter, and to make a difference.

Are you committed to have your life count, to make a difference, to matter?

Reviewing the Phoenix Myth Message

Recall that in the Phoenix Code, you start with the view, "This myth is about me and reveals who I really am."

The Phoenix refers to me—that means you are:

1. A unique creation with your own song to sing.

2. So powerful that you are able to alter the course of worldly events with your soul song.

3. Able to rise up in the face of the most devastating circumstances of life—such as aging, disease, financial meltdown, or natural disasters—and be triumphant.

What a powerful message. You matter! You make a difference! Sing! Your song is a splendid sun-stopping event.

The real message of the Phoenix Myth is still relevant today. It's a symbol of successfully rising above the ashes and disasters of life—not only as individuals, but also collectively as families, communities, countries, or humanity. It's about the opportunity to create and encourage each other to work together (in other words, to contribute to each other). If you are working on behalf of the planet's vulnerable children, you don't focus so much on yourself. If your game is to overcome the misery and insanity of war and to teach humanity to stop living in fear of each other, you won't spend your life figuring out about what brand of pretzels are the best.

The Transformation from Getting to Giving

It was August 1995 and I had been self-absorbed in dealing with my recovery from a deadly stomach cancer. My whole world shifted when a doctor looked at me and said, "You have cancer!" My days were spent resting; my life was spent surviving. I have since become amazed at the power of such pronouncements to cause resignation, regardless of whether you really have a disease.

Living in a small trailer with my wife and son, my world had shrunk into a very limiting space. My self-expression was confined, suppressed, and withheld. My finances were destroyed. Our marital relationship was dead. The future was nonexistent, and the present was nothing more than fearful, negative thinking. I couldn't even imagine how to save myself.

Suddenly I saw an opening. I could shift my game. Instead of trying to get love, health, peace of mind, and happiness, I could contribute, serve, and make a difference. Having been a teacher most of my life, I looked to see what I could share, teach, and instruct that would lift others. I got on the phone with a dear friend, Jinendra Jain, and asked if I could use my previous experience to help him teach communication courses around the world. After several conversations in which I assured him that I was committed to make a difference and that I would not simply abandon the effort at the first difficulty, he accepted me as a communication course leader with Landmark

Education, an organization that is a leader in personal development and transformative education.

Instantly my life shifted. Soon we were in a house I bought with my G. I. loan. I started to consult and make money, and my wife excelled at a world-class level in the martial arts. Life opened up again for us.

If you want to surpass your present level regardless of your age, live with more quality, experience new aliveness in your life, escape from being trapped in your mind, then seek to find a way to serve and get into action.

The German physician Albert Schweitzer took this to the ultimate when he left his prosperous practice in Germany and made his life about contributing his medical skills to remote African tribes. He devoted his life to providing healthcare for the African people, and in the process made a life of peace and satisfaction for himself. Later in his life, he wrote an open letter to humanity in which he said, "I don't know what your destiny will be, but one thing I know: the only ones among you who will be really happy are those who will have sought and found how to serve."

Neil Moore was a businessman in Australia who decided his unique song was the unusual way he learned to play piano quickly as a child without years of struggle. He decided to sing his unique song (his contribution to the world) by training children to learn to play the piano with his distinctive method. Through the years he has encouraged and led increasingly more people of all ages in mastering the piano with joy and without struggle. His company, Simply Music, continues to move into other countries and now includes instruments other than the piano. He is transforming music education worldwide with his staff of hundreds of teachers. A brilliant composer, a fully self-expressed musician, and an ever-expanding leader of a new paradigm for musical education, he is a perfect example of service and contribution.

In the summer of 1999, I walked into Mother Theresa's house of the dying in Kathmandu. A group of Westerners were just leaving. They came to assist with the dying of the poorest of the poor and had been there only two days but were asked to leave because they could not just **be** with the dying, destitute occupants of the mission. They felt they had to do something—fix things, make positive statements—but the dying simply needed someone to be with them. They needed compassion, not pity. They needed presence, not an agenda.

The Westerners who came to contribute were very confused when they were asked to leave. But the thing that was needed most by the dying—someone to be with—was something that most of those Westerners were unable to give.

You can make a difference and contribute simply by being willing to be with others. Be with them fully with no agenda of your own. Be there without needing to look good, do the right thing, or be appreciated; instead, just be fully present.

Giving others what they want is a simple way to make a difference. The people in your life want someone to be with. They may not want your advice, your good ideas, your opinions, your beliefs. Instead, they may want someone to just be with them.

Another way you can make a difference—to contribute to others—is to listen. Listen for the message of someone else's song. This is deeper than just hearing; real listening involves re-creating what someone else is saying with nothing added and nothing left out. That doesn't happen if you're thinking about what you're going to say. Listening requires letting go of *Me* and my point of view in favor of being fully present and looking into another's world to really see what is occurring. This takes some practice. One way is to interact with another by saying, "I would like to make sure I am getting what you are saying. What I hear you saying is ..." In this way, you can make sure you are really listening to the other person as the conversation between you unfolds.

You might choose to contribute with your art, music, sports, or dance. If you are fully expressing who you really are, you could say that you're "in the zone." You can serve others under any circumstance and in any condition. Even if you are sick, you can serve others by allowing them to contribute to you.

Can you even contribute when things aren't working for you?

One of my favorite examples of extraordinary contribution is Sidney Rittenberg, a translator who stayed in China following World War II. Even after the other Americans left, he stayed on, committed to being a bridge between China and the United States. A lone American in the Chinese world, he stood for making a difference in the face of two countries that were drifting apart. He took it upon himself to continue the presence of America in the Chinese culture, working in broadcasting and other forms of media.

On the night of February 27, 1968, a Chinese security detail came for him. He was put in prison where he remained for fifteen years, much of it in solitary confinement. When he was finally released from prison, he was healthy, free of bitterness and animosity toward the Chinese people. How did he do it? How did he survive this terrible experience?

He decided even while he lost access to his books and loved ones, he could still make a difference in prison by bridging the gap between his Chinese jailers and America. He could create, within the limits available to him, the bridge he was committed to building between China and America.

He shared stories with guards and talked to them about America. He reminded himself each day, "I matter, I am making a difference." That's not to say he had an easy time of it. Each day, he said, "I woke with the crushing realization that I am here in jail," but still he created a kind of freedom within the limits available to him. He kept his cell spotless and clean. He lived life to the fullest available to him. He became famous throughout China for his generous soul, his ability to rise above his circumstances.

Now over ninety, he is a business consultant for American companies that are considering doing business in China. He is the only American to have lived in China through all of that country's cultural revolutions and the evolution of Communism from World War II to 2012. As an American, he has a unique first-hand perspective on how the Chinese government has evolved over time.

When speaking about how he survived his experience so well, he says, "We all have far more power than we realize to have our life matter regardless of the circumstances in which we find ourselves."

If your life is only about your life, your personal entertainment, and your own amusements, you will pay the price of never having a great life. People like Nelson Mandela, Gandhi, Grandma Moses, Werner Erhard, Florence Nightingale, Jack LaLanne, Mother Theresa, Albert Einstein, Golda Meir, Stephen Hawking, Abraham Lincoln, and others like them have made (and make) their lives about something bigger than their life. They devote their life to contribution, and so can you and I.

Finding Your Unique Immortal Song—How You Can Make a Difference

When I know who I am, I am you.
When I don't know who I am, I serve you.
When I serve you, I discover I am you.

—Hunaman the Monkey God talking to Ram, Lord of the Universe, from the ancient Sanskrit epic the Ramayana

To begin, speculate what futures might be worth committing your life to. If you read the newspapers for a week, you will see that humanity has some huge issues, concerns, and problems that need to be resolved. The Phoenix message of new beginnings, greater accomplishment, and "we can do it" is needed more now than ever.

If you take action, you will find you count. As one who makes a difference, you are ageless. You can contribute. All of us, like the Phoenix Myth itself, can inspire each other to create new beginnings—new levels of life working for ourselves, others, and future generations. Contributing and serving is the Phoenix Myth in action.

As the great English playwright and philosopher George Bernard Shaw said:

This is the true joy in life, the being used for a purpose recognized by yourself as a mighty one; the being a force of nature instead of a feverish, selfish little clod of ailments and grievances, complaining that the world will not devote itself to making you happy.

I am of the opinion that my life belongs to the whole community, and as long as I live it is my privilege to do for it whatever I can.

I want to be thoroughly used up when I die, for the harder I work, the more I live. I rejoice in life for its own sake. Life is no brief candle to me; it is a sort of splendid torch which I have got hold of for the moment, and I want to make it burn as brightly as possible before handing it on to the future generations.

Actions

1. Review the Seven Keys of the Phoenix Myth and generate a plan to apply each one in your life. The more detailed you can make it the better.

2. After considering those things that are going on around you, determine which issues or problems you are really passionate about resolving.

3. Make a list of ways you could serve that would make a difference. Nothing is too small, nothing is too large.

4. From your list, select one or two ways that you could make a difference and get into action.

PART IV

Being a Phoenix

FUNDAMENTAL TO THE AGELESS LIFE is health, well-being, and unpredictable levels of accomplishment. The next two chapters provide a conversation and exercises that will empower you to go forward in these areas.

Chapter fifteen addresses a critical area for an ageless life. Very few people can enjoy ageless living when experiencing pain or ill health. This chapter is committed to providing you with information that allows you to be cause in the area of energy and health.

The next chapter on Impossible Games™, while introducing a practice for extraordinary results in any area of life, also has the advantage of providing you with a structure for sustaining your commitment to an ageless life.

Engaging with the material in Part IV will leave you naturally being a phoenix, i.e. being ageless.

CHAPTER 15

Building New Energy and Health for an Ageless Life

We are not victims of aging, sickness and death.
These are part of scenery, not the seer,
who is immune to any form of change.
This seer is the spirit, the expression of eternal being.

— Deepak Chopra

Ageless Health and Well-Being

WHILE HEALTH, ENERGY, AND WELL-BEING are not part of the Phoenix Myth, they are critical to a glorious, fulfilling life at any age. That's only natural, because the thing that is aging—our physical body—has a time span. Whereas, your self is eternal and ageless.

Is it possible, then, to have some control over our level of energy and health as our body gets older? Or do we just have to wait around and see what the cosmic lottery deals us? It's now common knowledge that our lifestyle choices and actions impact our health and well-being. Here's what that means: Whatever your current condition, you probably can influence your vitality, energy, and aliveness.

Many things help determine your health and well-being—but I believe that we have some control over about 80 percent of it. Perhaps, genetics play some role—but, more important is whether you are you willing to say you have the power to determine how much you are going to weigh, how much physical activity you will participate in, and what level of energy you will have. Action has the power to override genetics. You'll have the greatest amount of power over your health if you truly believe that you have a say about the degree of health you will enjoy. If you take full responsibility and live as if you are the cause of your energy, you have the maximum leverage regarding your health. You have choices, and what you choose matters.

Consider the design of the human body and its energy systems. There is considerable evidence from around the world that health and energy are affected by mental attitude, emotions, stress, nutrition, hydration, sleep, exercise, relationships, family, satisfaction at work, play, laughter, having fun, creative endeavors, and spiritual activity.

What you do matters. As an example, consider a UCLA study conducted that examined members of The Church of Jesus Christ of Latter-day Saints (Mormons), people who actively participate in the spiritual dimensions of their church. In this study, the research team found that the average lifespan of practicing Mormons is eleven years longer than that of non-Mormons in the United States. Eleven years. That's a huge deviation from the average.

How important is it for you to take action? Consider pollution. Most of us now live in deeply contaminated environments. The air in many cities is filthy. The West Coast presently has concerns about radiation fallout from Japan's recent nuclear reactor disasters. Our water supply is compromised with chlorine, fluorides, and runoff from agricultural chemicals and pesticides. In addition, there has been a major increase in the legal and illicit drugs we are ingesting, all of which to one degree or another are poisonous. One of the results of this pollution is a dramatic increase in cancer. It is now estimated in Western society that one of every two men and one of every three women will get cancer during their lifetime.

The TV Solution to "Health"

It is no accident that TV is filled with ads for medications to treat the pain and illness experienced by ever-expanding numbers of people. These ads are required by law to note the side effects caused by their products—and you've undoubtedly noticed that the side effects are often worse than any symptoms you are bothered by.

What happens then? You'll need more drugs to deal with the breakdowns caused by your previous round of "medications." It's easy to see that medication is just another misleading name for drugs—poisonous substances your body has to somehow eliminate. Taking even more poisons to feel better is true insanity!

You cannot count on the normal medical model of our culture to provide the highest level of health and well-being, because it's a model based on dealing with symptoms instead of promoting the building blocks of great health and preventative medicine.

Altering Your Biological Age

What can you do to dramatically alter your chronological age? Other than lying about it, there's nothing you can do to change your chronological age. But you can impact the *biological age* of your body. There are eighty-year-old men and women who have bodies as biologically sound as that of a forty-year-old—and, on the flip side, there are forty-year-old men and women with bodies biologically as old as that of an eighty-year-old.

Your health and energy results from some basic elements:

- Good nutrition, including sufficient pure water and clean air
- Exercise and movement
- Avoidance of toxins and poisons
- Freedom from excessive stress
- Sufficient rest and sleep
- And, most important, bliss—doing what you love to do in life

Altering Your Biological Age—The Difference Food Makes

A good place to start in the quest for health and wellness is with what you eat. "The China Study," a large research project on the nutritional habits of the people of China conducted by T. Colin Campbell, investigated what people in different regions ate. The study suggested a definitive correlation between what people ate and the diseases from which they died. Campbell made a compelling argument for a direct relationship between diet and disease—especially a correlation between eating meat and dairy and rising death rates from cancer, diabetes, and other major illnesses.

On the other hand, indigenous Eskimo populations existed on 80 percent fat and 20 percent protein—with virtually no fruit or vegetables in their diet. Yet they had a very low incidence of cardio vascular disease and cancers, something that held true until the last fifty years. In recent times, though, few Eskimos eat their traditional diets—and with the adoption of engineered and packaged foods, their health and well-being have plummeted. In case you think the Eskimos are somehow a rare exception, consider Africa's Maasai tribe—those that follow the diet of their ancestors, consisting primarily of raw milk and cattle blood, are extremely healthy. In other words, humans have adapted to a variety of diets—and to ignore that is to ignore what may bring you a higher degree of nutritional excellence.

With meat, in particular red meat, as well as with dairy products it's wise to consider the diet of the animals whose fluids or meats are eaten. We might seriously question what chemicals, hormones, antibiotics, and other unnatural practices are now being used in the raising of animals you eat. It seems that unconscionable animal husbandry methods, by and large based on greed, have become the norm in the meat and dairy factory farm industry.

Of critical consideration is how the animals you eat are being housed and fed. In many cases, animals are caged and kept in the dark; they are kept in overcrowded spaces, and in some cases their feet are cut off. All those conditions have a profound impact on the health of animals. Consider their diets: Many animals are fed foods they normally would not eat. Grain is substituted for grass, and the meat from diseased animals is fed to pigs and cattle. Anything that impacts the well-being of the animal will also in some way negatively impact your health and well-being. You can become sick and even die as a result of eating containmated meat.

You can reduce your risks by choosing wild game or animals naturally raised, without hormones or artificial feeds. I recommend the meat of only those animals that have been raised on their natural diet and are labeled organic.

Another industry under scrutiny for its negative impact on human health is the fish farming trade. These so-called fish farms are in actuality tanks. The fish are usually overcrowded and often get diseased. Antibiotics are then added to their feed, a practice that has a negative impact on their health. Fish are also being fed what they would not eat in nature, including the dead bodies of other animals. In addition, heavy metal toxins—such as mercury, cadmium, PCBs, and lead, all of which cause cancer and brain damage—have been detected in harmful concentrations in the fish raised in most fish farms. These heavy metal toxins in the cells of the farmed fish are later consumed by humans in dangerous amounts. The result is more incidents of cancer, cardio problems, diabetes, and other major diseases.

Many doctors recommend dietary supplements of omega-3 fish oils to ensure cardiovascular and brain health. But consider this: Exercise is what produces a high quality of omega-3 in fish oil—and when farmed fish are jammed into overcrowded fish tanks that prevent any sort of exercise, the quality of omega-3 in their oil is very low.

If you can't find wild fish caught in waters that are tested and proved to be free of toxins—waters like those in the Pacific Northwest, New Zealand, Australia, and Iceland—don't eat fish. A growing number of restaurants use only meat from naturally grown animals and fish caught in the wild. When you eat out, ask! If enough people refuse to eat animal factory meat and fish from fish farms, such practices will cease to exist. Consumers drive industries. You vote with your dollars.

Some experts in the field of nutrition recommend that we eat fresh, whole, organic plant foods. Don't automatically fall for an "organic" label on food. Take care to select foods with no added pesticides, dyes, flavors, genetic modification, inorganic fertilizers, and other engineering. Remember that many foods are often adulterated; for example, the "butter" put on popcorn at the movie theater isn't real butter—it's a chemically engineered substitute oil often rancid.

You can't stay healthy as you age if you ignore the fact that our food supply is deeply compromised. We could write a whole book on genetically modified and engineered foods that are designed to be addictive but compromise our health. The increase of processed, packaged food includes a corresponding decrease in healthy, natural produce. Don't think you can compensate for that trend by consuming synthetic vitamin pills, supplements, and fractionalized food elements, much of which goes undigested.

What you put in your body is a choice with huge consequences. As your body gets older, you especially need to be more selective regarding the fuel you put in it for maximum energy. Many experts make this simple recommendation—***eat real food***! Eat more of your food raw. Eat organic fruits and vegetables every day. Eat whole-plant foods that are grown without added chemicals or unneeded processing. Read labels and be aware of what you are putting into your body.

Simply put, what worked in the past no longer works. If you want optimum health, you must become more aware of the source of what you eat. Grow your own food or find reliable access to natural food sources like local farmers' markets. Search for food that will promote your best health and optimum energy.

Restricting calories is one way to extend lifespan, and it's a fairly simple task to accomplish: Simply eat fewer calories. This is where real, living food comes in—it provides greater nutrition and fewer empty calories, leading to optimum health, vitality, and high performance as we age. Carrying less body fat and weight—even less than the commonly accepted and falsely elevated norms of Western society—will probably result in greater health and energy for most of us.

For the last few years, carbohydrates have gotten a very bad rap. That reputation is deserved when it comes to refined carbohydrates. But many experts suggest that whole grains not only provide dense nutrition, but also add bulk and fiber, which in turn reduce hunger and cravings.

I also find that my energy stays strong throughout the day if I eat smaller amounts about five times a day. This practice also keeps metabolism high, which helps keep weight stable.

Here are some general suggestions for your nutrition management:

- Include in your diet more natural fresh foods with rich nutrition and fewer calories, like raw fruits and vegetables—preferably organic.
- Eliminate unreal food, such as packaged snacks, candies; products that contain fructose, sugar,

and chemical concoctions (read the label); and genetically modified or engineered "foods." Virtually all products in the center aisles of the grocery store fall into these categories. Avoid foods that have oils added. These often go rancid and contain preservatives, insecticides, and artificial colors. Don't expect to find any real food at movie theaters or convenience stores.

- Drink at least one quart of pure water every day. Eliminate soda and bottled or packaged fruit juice drinks.

- Dramatically reduce or entirely eliminate the amount of dairy in your diet; if you do use dairy, opt for naturally fed cattle and unpasteurized milk, which now is considered best by leading-edge nutritionists.

Finally, what is your number-one nutritional enemy? Sugar! Avoid it! Read the statistics regarding the explosion of obesity, diabetes, and other dreaded diseases in this country, and you'll find they are directly correlated to the increased use of sugar and refined carbohydrates (white bread turns into mostly sugar in the digestive process).

So, if you want to eliminate the most important health threat first, avoid pure cane sugar and all its relatives—maltodextrin, organic cane juice, sucrose, fructose, and high-fructose corn syrup (sugar is often purposely concealed with names not commonly recognized). These inexpensive varieties of sugar began being added to products about twenty-five years ago. Today, sugar in one of its forms is in virtually every packaged or refined "food" that you purchase.

Keep in mind that sugar is addictive—and food manufacturers have had you coming back for more since you were a baby. Most of us have no idea about the tremendous money, lobbying, and massive manipulation to keep us in the dark about the detrimental effects revealed in study after study from the large amounts of sugar being consumed.

If you'd like to learn more, seek out some of the world's masters in the world of health and nutrition who can mentor you in your growth and development.

Altering Your Biological Age—The Power of Exercise

I believe the best strategy for reducing your biological age is exercise. Consider the example of Russian heart doctor Nikolay Amosov, who scientifically investigated methods to slow down the biological process of aging. At the age of sixty-five, as he began to decline in health and energy, he decided to fight back. He used his medical background to intensify his research into the human body's aging mechanisms, and he became doggedly determined to combat the debilitating effects of aging.

Amosov developed and proved an anti-aging theory with experiments involving intense physical exercise. After inventing a system requiring thousands of daily movements, he added jogging and walking to the regimen. Even though he had a serious heart condition and a pacemaker, he demonstrated the efficacy of his method through his own improved health, energy, and strength.

He increased his daily physical exercises up to a phenomenal 2,500 repetitions, half of which were done with dumbbells weighing as much as twelve pounds. Later, he redoubled the number of exercise movements to 5,000 repetitions. As a result, he experienced a strong reversal of the common symptoms associated with aging and dramatically improved his levels of energy, health, and function. He subsequently wrote a best-selling book, *Overcoming Aging*, which described his findings.

After corrective heart surgery, he immediately re-engaged in his exercise regimen, which included an hour a day of walking, either indoors or outdoors. He gradually expanded the amount and level of his exercise, and again his physical debilitation gave way to strength and vitality. He slowly increased his exercise repetitions back up to 3,000. He even jogged, mostly downhill. Throughout his nineties, he persevered in his program, walking every day throughout his city. For the rest of his life he was able to travel alone and with ease on planes, trains, and buses. In spite of his heart defects, a pacemaker, replacement heart valves, and shunts, he lived to the age of ninety-four—alive and strong, blazing the trail for the rest of us.

Amosov's beginning recommendations are the same for everyone—thirty to forty-five minutes of stretching and physical strengthening exercises. Such a regimen will consist of 1,000 to 1,500 movements, including 500 repetitions with dumbbells as heavy as twelve pounds. In addition, he recommends one hour of intensive walking daily—or, even more effective, three kilometers of jogging a day.

Amosov advises that men and women over the age of fifty double this regimen. He says it is important to exercise responsibly and use caution, increasing the intensity of the exercises gradually—no more than 3 percent per day. He also recommends that you monitor and control your pulse rate, which he asserts should not generally exceed 120 if you're over the age of fifty and not normally exceed a rate of 140 if younger.

If you have any heart problems or other physical infirmities, do this program in coordination with a physician. Work slowly to double your rate of physical training.

Don't want to exercise? Then prepare to participate in the decline of aging by default. Vital health and agelessness demand lifestyle changes of new action. Biological age regression has a price; with every gift comes responsibility.

I assert that exercise and movement of the body on a regular basis is absolutely critical to living an ageless life. Super ager Jack Lalanne still worked out three to four hours a day at the age of ninety-five. He demonstrated the power of exercise and its impact on the biological age of the body.

I met Jack when I was working out at Norman Marks Gym in Oakland, California. He was surprisingly short, but what a dynamo of energy. To be with him was to be inspired by who he was being—passionate, alive, and present. Jack Lalanne demonstrated for all of us that action in the world of health produces results.

First Steps To Reverse Your Biological Age

A human body is like any other good machine—it works best with the correct fuel, good care, and maintenance. Here are some simple first steps you can take to improve your biological age and your experience of being ageless:

- Engage in variety of exercises, such as strength training, cardio, physical games, stretching exercises, endurance training, and core exercises.

- Follow good health habits; don't use tobacco, and if you drink, drink only on rare occasions and then only in moderation. Alcohol is not a health food! Reduce or eliminate the consumption of caffeine.

- Avoid the use of drugs both legal and illegal. Allopathic drugs have a detrimental effect, damaging fundamental vitality, health, and the function of our cells and our body systems.

- Reduce your stress. It is believed that most illness results from stress. Exercise, good nutrition, and daily meditation all reduce stress.

- Spiritual practices, as well as learning and mastering new domains of knowledge and skills, are fundamental to aliveness and health, and also reduce stress.

- Make sure you drink plenty of clean, pure water without added chemicals. Drink at least one quart a day. At birth, our bodies are 95 percent water, and we slowly dry up throughout life. A well-hydrated brain is essential for clear thinking; when dehydrated, the brain operates at less than 70 percent efficiency. Fight back—drink water!

- Start to supplement your daily diet with fresh vegetable and fruit juices, which are concentrated real foods. Everyone needs a good juicer. Use vegetables and fruits that have been raised organically to juice.

- A great place to begin to improve your nutrition is to eat at least one healthy meal every day; breakfast is a good one to start with. Your meal should be nutritious, natural, healthy, and loaded with vitamins and minerals.

The following is a general recipe for a Phoenix power breakfast. It was developed at the "Transforming the Myth of Aging" course that we conducted in Sundance, Utah. Use fresh and organic ingredients whenever possible; feel free to modify the recipe according to your own taste. We recommend using a quality blender like a Vitamix or Blendtec for the best results.

1. Begin with any dry ingredients you want to use, such as flax seeds, cacao nibs, cacao beans, or nuts; and grind them to your desired consistency.

2. Add a base liquid, such as coconut water, preferably from a fresh (green) young coconut; fresh juice you make yourself (such as carrot, apple, grape, or celery juice); or pure water.

3. Add your favorite items from this list but keep it simple—don't mix too many things together:
   - Coconut meat from your coconut
   - Greens, such as spinach, kale, chard, broccoli, or sprouts
   - Cucumber
   - Avocado
   - Tomato
   - Supplements, such as Dr. Schulze's SuperFood Plus

- Seaweed (this is best with vegetable-based smoothies)
- Herbs or spices, such as cinnamon or sea salt
- Fresh lemon and/or lime (without peel)

4. Thin with additional liquid if needed.

A powerful green smoothie!

Actions

1. Take the opportunity now to determine whether your current actions are consistent with your values and self-interest in the area of health and well-being.

   - In the area of nutrition, my main daily practices are ...
   - In the area of exercise, my weekly pattern is ...
   - In the domain of spirituality, my actions are ...
   - I am developing myself mentally by ...

2. Eat a Phoenix power breakfast each day for a week. Graph your daily energy level on a scale of one to ten to track your improved energy levels.

CHAPTER 16

Impossible Games™—Challenges that Make You Younger

The secret of life is to have a task,
something you devote your entire life to,
something you bring everything to,
every minute of the day for your whole life.
And the most important thing is, it must be
something you cannot possibly do!

— Henry Moore

I F YOU FAIL TO CREATE, you will experience the decline of aging by default. For most, it's not possible to escape the ordinary decline of aging by will alone. Instead, you have to act to get the greatest results.

Human beings are called into extraordinary performance in the challenge of a great game. That holds true for aging as well: You need an empowering context and an engaging game that will enliven you and call you to play.

You can create and play an Impossible Game™ in any area of life, but it must be something that, at first, you are certain you cannot accomplish. Regardless of whether you win, just playing an Impossible Game™ whole-heartedly—as if it were possible—will take you to unimaginable accomplishment beyond your known limits. The prospect of succeeding in your Impossible Game™ must excite and thrill you. The challenge may seem to be overwhelming at times, yet you will feel most alive even in the struggle.

The human body is one of the most productive areas in which to create an Impossible Game™. Our minds definitely establish limitations that seem real regarding our physical bodies. But you can expand your physical performance at any age and at any time if you're determined enough.

It's time to blow your mind! The following inquiry will move you into the arena or space in which Impossible Games™ are played. Imagine a physical feat that seems impossible for you. You could take on winning a dance championship even if you are not a dancer. You could take on running a marathon if you are not a runner. You could take on an ultra-marathon if you have already run a marathon. You could take on moving a finger if you are paralyzed. The important part is to choose a game that you cannot now imagine is possible for you to win.

Exercise

Design an Impossible Game™ in the area of your health and well-being. It will serve as the foundation for your aliveness and for transformation of all the areas of your life.

Some Examples:

- I will win a ballroom dance competition within one year.
- I will get my blood pressure below 120/80 within three months.
- I will run a marathon by December 25.
- I will participate in a 100-mile bike race by the end of August.
- I will do a triathlon before May 1.
- I will spend three weeks hiking on the Appalachian Trail by next June.
- I will do a 5-mile ocean swim by the end of this year.
- I will do a 5K run within 6 months.

Once you choose your game, get clear about what you will need to win. One of the most essential resources you may require is a great coach. When your mind argues that you can't do it, your coach is the one who will tell you that you can and that you will. Your coach creates a game plan with you and provides a structure for taking sufficient, consistent, and right action in order to accomplish your intended outcome.

Want an example? My friend Garrett White leveraged Impossible Games™ in a remarkable way. He went from being able to run five miles on a treadmill to doing three-hundred-mile races. And he transformed his body and mind in the process. As he plays Impossible Games™, he inspires all who know him.

The toughest race in America—The Badwater. For me and many others, this was and is an Impossible Game™ to play.

Finding Your Impossible Game™

1. What are some of your favorite physical activities? Which one gives you a special jolt of aliveness when you imagine mastering it? You might enjoy swimming, walking, dancing, skiing, bowling, running, biking, yoga, strength training, or martial arts, for example. Consider all games, even if you've never participated in them. You could even invent a new game—there are no limits!

2. Are there any physical games in which you are now engaged? Keep in mind that a game exists within a specific period of time and has clear intended outcomes that determine whether you win or lose. A game has a specific ending time.

3. If you could accomplish anything in the physical domain, what would you choose? Create a game in which you actually could accomplish that.

4. Have you ever thought something was physically impossible and later discovered you were able to do it? What was it? What characteristic enabled you to accomplish it?

5. What steps did you go through to accomplish that seemly impossible result?

6. Is there a physical goal that you would really love to accomplish but haven't even started because you've been stopped by fear of failure, looking foolish, or of even imagining that you could succeed. What would you love to do that seems impossible?

7. What new adventures can you imagine in the physical domain that touch your passion and inspire you?

8. Where in the domain of health and well-being are you playing smaller, more comfortable games, excusing yourself from living your greatest physical ambitions and dreams? What do you say about yourself in the domain of physicality? Is it true?

Using what you discovered above, write and say the following statements to yourself:

- Based on declaration alone, without regard to the circumstances or to what is commonly considered possible, I now declare as possible the impossible physical game of _____.

- My intended outcome is _____. (An intended outcome details your deadline and how you will know you have won your game.)

- I now generate the following new beliefs about my power and ability to win my game:

- My coach, support team, or network will be:

- The new habits, knowledge, and skills I will acquire for my victory are:

- I choose to play this game because:

- The outcomes and new possibilities for my future that would be gained from playing and winning this impossible physical game are:

Game Plan

It's important to write down what action you will take, when you will take it, and whether someone else is involved. Who is that person? Begin with the first action and work forward in time; for example, plan and write down what will you do today, tomorrow, next week. List just the critical actions—in other words, those actions that are critical to realizing your intended result.

To get started, write down the first critical actions you will take:

What?   When?   Who?

As you move forward in your game, you will need to create additional action plans.

Now write down some of the details of your game:

- These are the strengths I will need to develop to accomplish my game:

- These are the resources and support that will forward my game:

- This is who I will be when I have won my impossible game:

Now move the game you have designed from a plan into reality. Begin to take the actions you have delineated, and visualize succeeding until your Impossible Game™ appears possible.

The Power of an Impossible Game™

Remember that an Impossible Game™ can include a game you invent that you could never win but are willing to play with all your might and determination as if you could win it.

For example, I know a woman who, as an ordinary forty-six-year-old, created the Impossible Game™ of winning an Olympic gold medal. Along the way, she went from being a middle-aged, overweight, out of shape, mildly depressed, average American homemaker to becoming a world champion in the martial arts—and she did it at an age that everyone considered was too old. In 2010, at the age of sixty-seven, she was still playing her Impossible Game™ and became a U. S. National Taekwondo Technical Team Member, competing in a sport against people of all ages—most of them forty years younger than she.

She played her Impossible Game™ first in her mid-forties, then in her fifties, and still played it in her sixties.

She has developed incredible flexibility, strength, speed, stamina, and balance—words that are not usually spoken in the same sentence with the word grandmother! She won nine world titles after the age of fifty. She trained with the U. S. Olympic team in full-contact Taekwondo in the year 2000.

I highly recommend that you watch the story of her Impossible Game™ on YouTube™—you can find it with the search term "*iology* Mary Louise Zeller Story Emotional Fingerprint."

I don't simply know of her—I know her well. Mary Louise is my wife and partner. She is now taking on an Impossible Game™ in the domain of money and finances, and she is winning again! I hardly recognize her; she hardly recognizes herself. When she decided to take on a network marketing opportunity, my first thought was, "What a waste of time and money!" I have had to eat those words a thousand times! Five years later, she has created financial independence for our family and others and is a world leader in the industry.

This was a woman who used to tell me, "Oh, honey, you are so very good at making money and I am so very good at spending it. I don't see a problem." She never balanced her bank account or paid the bills. Now she handles finances better than an accountant. I feel like I have a new wife, and her transformation keeps me falling in love with her over and over. As I write this, Mary Louise, at the age of seventy, is the perfect example of living an ageless life.

When you play your Impossible Game™ you will give yourself a dramatic increase in energy, health, vitality, and performance. You will also undoubtedly build a body of power and beauty—a body you will love. People will say, "I can't believe how great you look; you look ten years younger! How are you doing it?" Of course you will say, "I Phoenixed myself" and then refer them to:

RonZeller.com

Like the fabled Phoenix, you will be an inspiration to those who see that for your age, you have dramatic vitality and beauty.

Actions

Create, plan, and start to play your Impossible Game™ in the physical domain.

What's Next for You?—
Creating Your Phoenix Future

This is it!
— Werner Erhard

How to Live Your Ageless Life Now

IN BRINGING FORTH your ageless Phoenix life, you will naturally access new levels of success. We call the transformation you will realize the Phoenix Effect. It's easy to invent and create a new life; it's not easy to follow through on your creation, overcome the obstacles, and manifest the results that surpass your ordinary limitations. In fact, very few people successfully do it. In order to accomplish such a transformation, you must be willing to live with integrity and respect your word, the word with which you spoke your possibility into existence.

How do you break free of your self-imposed limitations and normal ways of being? Part of the answer is to create a powerful future—a future that is so inspiring and uplifting that it impacts your actions in the present. To realize this new future, you'll need to become a fully engaged, brand new person. Another part of the answer is to shift the context from which you are living life. Your Impossible Game™ delivers a whole new context from which to live.

A worker in Egypt building a pyramid could have had the context of laboring endlessly, moving and cutting large blocks of stone. In contrast, he could have had the context of building a glorious tomb for the pharaoh—a place from which the pharaoh could contact the gods and rescue the worker, his family, and his people. The quality of the builder's work and his satisfaction depended on his context, which gave rise to his perception and interpretation.

What is your life going to be about? In the Phoenix Myth, the Phoenix is said to have a unique song—a song so beautiful that even the sun stopped in its flight across the heavens to listen. Your career, contribution, and soul purpose are expressions of your unique song. Your unique song is the context that generates the power to realize your success, to make the rest of your life the best of your life. What is your soul purpose?

Creating Your Vision for an Ageless Life

As a way of bringing your vision forth, look at the following questions and write down your present answers.

What is my vision and mission for my ageless life?

Regarding my vision, what are the benchmarks or major outcomes along the way?

Now expand, refine, and clarify the details of your newly generated life vision. Design your Phoenix future in the following areas:

My vision of my newly rising Phoenix financial future is:

The major benchmarks of my financial future are:

Releasing the constrictions of your past-based experience, create a new vision of your social life. My vision of my new Phoenix social life is:

The major benchmarks of my social future are:

My vision of a Phoenix future in the domain of intimate relationships is:

To fulfill my vision for my intimate relationships, the major benchmarks are:

Review and Exercises for Getting the Most Out of This Book

1. Literally *choose and speak* agelessness into existence. Create being ageless; thereafter, have only those conversations with yourself and others that are consistent with being ageless. It is truly a choice.

2. Create a new mindset; shift from a world of reaction and helplessness to a world of awesome power and creation. Your access to an ageless life occurs through engaging in your power to create. You are a creator. When you are engaged in conscious creation, you are ageless. We are always engaged in creation, either unconsciously or consciously. You choose—you can live the myth of aging or you can enter a new World of Ageless Living.

3. Identify the disempowering attitudes and points of view that you have created. Which ones are you willing to let go? Like a Phoenix, create being complete with the past.

4. Create new beliefs about yourself and others. You created the ones you have now. You have the power; use it to create greatness.

5. Own your power to **name**. Be aware of what you have named yourself and others. Invent conversations and names that empower you, others, and life. Name yourself as one who makes a difference and contributes to life.

6. Clear out, clean up, organize, and design your physical space so that it is aligned with your **Portal to Being**. Your environment then reminds you of who you really are and becomes the reality system for a whole new way of being. Start a journey of creating beauty in all your physical environments.

7. Design and plan a new life for yourself—a life that includes playing and mastering an Impossible Game™. This will be the source of your never-ending expansion.

8. Take on the commitment of creating extraordinary energy, health, aliveness, and performance. Eat for aliveness and energy, using live, real foods and nutritionally dense super foods.

9. Create an Impossible Game™ in the domain of physical well-being and engage in the practice of strengthening your body through intensive exercise. Create a game plan and a support structure for your Impossible Game™, get a coach, and play to win within a certain time frame.

Creating New Space

The three areas below are designed to be mastered over time. Take on one aspect from one of these areas each week, intending to have a breakthrough.

1. Enter the space of prosperity by:
   - Discovering ways to create value for other people. Find new ways to help, heal, and empower others.
   - Examining your willingness to be prosperous. Some people are really good at giving value but terrible at receiving it. If you are unwilling to receive, then others are blocked and thwarted in their desire to be generous and make a difference. Flow occurs as you give and take.

2. Clear out and clean up your inner space by:
   - Completing things from the past through forgiveness. In particular, forgive yourself and others.
   - Generating love for yourself as well as others.
   - Completing any resentments or regrets you have through communication with others.
   - Killing the ANTs. Most people's minds are infested with ANTs (automatic negative thoughts) about themselves and others; these

thoughts often have nothing to do with reality. Recognize this phenomenon as merely a default human mechanism, and consciously choose to create empowering conversations about you and others.

3. Practice integrity by:
   - Continuing to look for situations in which your integrity is out of balance. Persistently restore your integrity, including places in which integrity is missing in your physical environment.
   - Giving up compromise. Where are you compromising your fundamental principles, ideals, and values?

Congratulations! Thank you for allowing me to be your partner in the extraordinary creation of ageless life! Fly forth now into a new world and your ageless second half!

ACKNOWLEDGEMENTS

I thank the following people for their contribution to this work:

Dr. Nikolai Amosov, a Russian pioneer in exercise as an antidote to aging. His commitment to sharing his experiment the ageless possibility is truly inspiring.

Donna Bell for her unique distinctions in creating community by transforming physical environments and using radiating points to find one's true self.

Dr. Walter Bortz for his vast scholarly contribution to our understanding of aging.

Joseph Campbell, probably the world's foremost expert on myths and their relevance for our lives.

Werner Erhard, originator of the est training, Landmark Forum, and other powerful transformative programs. Werner is a pioneer in the exploration of the being of human beings, a champion for integrity, and the power of being our word instead of psychology.

Dr. Lillian Fodermaier for her contribution to planning and development of our Winning the Second Half courses.

Michael Jensen, a Harvard professor who along with Werner Erhard, stands for the impact of authenticity and integrity in life.

Jack Lalanne a model of living the ageless life. Jack inspired millions to cause health improvement and well-being through exercise and nutrition.

David Logan who has clearly laid out the power we each have through rhetoric to create with our word.

Yogananda, Sri Aurobindo, Sri Yukteswar, other Indian Masters, and yogis who have introduced new paradigms for each of us to move forward into ageless greatness.

Peter Zeller I have known you all your life. I appreciate and love you deeply brother. Thank you for the gift of family you bring me.

Art Eggertsen, developer of the ProBar and a source of nutrition education, whose food nurtured our course participants at Sundance in how to live an ageless life.

Pavel Tsatsouline, teacher and coach who has brought a new clarity to the field of physical fitness, physical culture, and cultivating the ageless body.

Joe Polish friend, mentor, source of constant contribution—the ultimate connector.

Roger Dillon my soul friend, confident, and brilliant student of life.

Mark Kamin my business partner of many years who stands for integrity in business, life, and relationships.

Berny Dohrmann a master at empowering all of those he meets. His CEO Space is a brilliant coaching structure for reaching our business aspirations quickly.

Dr. Dewayne Smith whose genius in mitochondria research saved my life.

Drs. Anna Maria & Brian Clement—whatever your illness, their Hippocrates Institute offers hope as well as a glimpse of the ageless life through nutrition and other heath restoration treatments.

Dr. Barry Morguelan who has brought the power of Chinese medicine to America in a generous, serving way. The hours we have spent together have blessed my family and I with healing and light.

Dr. Nick Gonzalez a part of my medical team that helped me deal with anything that came up in my brazen attempt to take being ageless from a concept to reality.

Harry Rosenberg CEO of Landmark Education and my partner in planetary transformation for many years now.

Julie Hall founder of Cherish Our Children International whose commitment to disadvantaged children creates miracles all over the planet in the lives of beautiful but often forgotten children. Starting with the overwhelming condition of the infamous Romanian orphanages, Julie's organization COCI has expanded ever since in service and goodness.

Neil and Hunter Moore two of my closest friends and real pioneers in creating the ageless life.

Dr. Norman Marks thanks for all those years of intensive weight training together.

Dave Copps friend and business partner. I'm looking forward to the resounding success of your company Pure Discovery.

Steve Sadaka thank you for your friendship down through the years. Thank you Steve for being willing to swim with sharks!

Joe and Betty Roza we really had a great time with Prime Quest; I've loved our adventures together. Joe I treasure our time together presenting the 6-day course.

Dr. Daniel Amen who made a huge contribution to my son Adam with his expertise in healing the brain.

To my mother, Olive Zeller, who proved that one can beat cancer no matter what the diagnosis. In the area of service, you have been my life long roll model as a governmental leader in the state of Wisconsin.

To my father, Peter Zeller, whose commitment to humanity took priority over political positioning. Thank you for your deep thinking and commitment for a vision of life that works for all of us. I love you dad.

Charlene Afremoe my partner in the game of transformation for decades. What a coach and teacher you are! What a difference in life you have made for hundreds of thousands worldwide.

John Assaraf who showed me how to win Impossible Games™ like being a world champion. You are such a great example of how to focus our mental powers.

Landon Carter whose empowerment and stand for me during the 6-day changed my direction for the rest of my life from a local to a worldwide educator.

Maggie and Michael Delia who allowed me to be their consultant and work together to transform their company.

Steward Esposito thanks for the many wonderful "intensives" we had together at est and Landmark reinventing ourselves.

Linda and Mike Higgins our adventures in weight lifting and Harley tours together have produced great moments in my life.

Sherrill Jeter has been a true partner for many years in taking transformation to many cultures and countries. We have spent real precious time together.

Kay and George Keeler thank you both for your generosity and contribution to my family and me. You endowed us with a very special chapter in life.

Acknowledgements

Dr. E. J. Raven the chiropractor's chiropractor, my body thanks you for the great work you do.

Steve Zaffron what a brilliant partner in the work of transformation you have been and are. Your book *The Three Laws of Performance* provides a quantum jump in the knowledge of how to transform companies.

Tony Robbins: Thanks, Tony, for coaching my wife Mary Louise to her first world championship in Taekwondo.

Grandmaster Joone Rhee a treasure to America and a father of TKW in the West. Thank you for suggesting that Mary Louise train with the US team for the 2000 Olympics. Thank you Grandmaster for your love for the American dream. You have inspired countless martial artists worldwide with your philosophy and teaching.

Bret Rhomer a real friend and partner in keeping the house repairs at Sundance under control.

Ruth Shinsel our talks opened up the possibility of the spiritual life for a geologist like me.

Glenda Shinsel my first wife who put up with me for six years and co-created three magnificent sons.

Barbara Ott we had fourteen great years together. Thanks Barbara for helping me raise those three sons, your friendship, companionship, and adventures together.

U.S. Marine Corp.—it is true, once a marine always a marine. The commitments to fitness and rigor have lived on and are still here with me at 80.

Dr. Keith Rigby my geology graduate degree advisor at Brigham Young University, who made a difference for human kind in understanding ancient sponges.

Joseph Mercola whose health newsletter inspires me and hundreds of thousands of others.

Master William Kim thank you for your belief in your older, out of shape student Mary Louise Zeller. Your faith and coaching resulted in her nine world championships and a shot at the Olympics. That was a real exciting possibility!

And finally Stephen Hawking who is one of the world's greatest demonstrations of living an ageless life—having your purpose trump your physicality.

There are so many others I haven't listed here that have contributed, inspired me, and trained me; nevertheless you are here in my heart.

And More...

For additional resources on living a Phoenix life, comments, or to communicate with me, please visit my website:

RonZeller.com

Made in the USA
Lexington, KY
30 June 2016